Making the Most of WriteItNow 4

D1303156

Making the Most of WriteItNow 4

by *Gary Lee Entsminger*
& Susan Elizabeth Elliott

PINYON PUBLISHING
MONTROSE, COLORADO

Cover painting copyright © 2010 by Susan E. Elliott
Cover and Book design by Susan E. Elliott

First Edition: 2010

Pinyon Publishing
23847 V66 Trail, Montrose, CO 81403
www.pinyon-publishing.com

Library of Congress Control Number: 2010924109
ISBN: 978-0-9821561-4-8

Special thanks...

to Rob Walton for his insightful comments on an earlier draft of this book.

Contents

EXPORTING & TIPS

WRITEITNOW ESSENTIALS

CHAPTER 1 Getting Started

> Sit at your desk for three hours each morning. Don't allow yourself to read, answer phone calls, tidy up, or anything else. You sit there. If you are not writing, you still sit there. Eventually, you will write.
>
> —Flannery O'Connor

WriteItNow makes Flannery O'Connor's mandate to sit and write less intimidating. It helps bring the fun back into writing. If you know what you want to write, WriteItNow helps you stay organized. If you're not sure what to write, WriteItNow inspires your creativity. When you've finished writing, WriteItNow gives you the tools you need to prepare and export your manuscript.

To help you make the most of WriteItNow, we'll walk you through the many WriteItNow features that can improve your writing experience.

About this Book

Although we can all benefit from a weekend writing workshop, most of us are too busy or can't afford to attend. But we can afford to buy or borrow a book. Think of this book as your surrogate WriteItNow Weekend Warrior Workshop. Ravenshead Services has supplied the software for your writing adventures, and we'll help you make the most of it.

We'll show you how to use WriteItNow to write your story or novel, from your first idea to final manuscript. We won't teach you how to write *per se* (that's your business), but we will show you how to use WriteItNow to develop your story, step by step.

Stories grow from inspiration, ideas, and notes. You create and develop characters that live in your story. As your story becomes more complex, WriteItNow becomes invaluable—making it easy for you to organize your work and visualize your progress. When you've finished writing, you can seamlessly export your story to a printer or to book design software. You can even transfer stories that you started in other word processors such as Microsoft Word into WriteItNow. Almost anything is possible.

Many of the WriteItNow features we cover are optional or advanced, and you might not have noticed them yet. For example, suppose you're having a morning of writer's block and need an idea to get you jump started. The Idea Generator can help. Or suppose you can't seem to find anything interesting to say about a character. WriteItNow's Create a Character from a Prompt can inspire you.

WriteItNow is really two programs: (1) a sophisticated word processor and story organizer and (2) a set of tools to help you improve your writing. We suggest you use this book as a step by step guide to using WriteItNow as well as a reference for the features in WriteItNow.

It's worth your while to thumb through this book before you get too far into your story. It will help you know what's available in WriteItNow and what's to come as your story gains momentum. Use the table of contents, the index at the end of this book, and the shaded page topics to locate information quickly.

We begin by describing essential knowledge you need to use WriteItNow (Chapters 1-2). We describe the structure of WriteItNow and how to move around the interface. We show you the basics of creating, saving, and loading WriteItNow story files (.wnw files).

Then in Chapters 3-6, we describe how WriteItNow contributes to sequential stages of the writing process: beginning, expanding, and enhancing your story. We show you, example by example, how to use WriteItNow tools and features. We apply those tools in an example story that we're writing, called "A Vision."

> *The very first thing I tell my new students on the first day of a workshop is that good writing is about telling the truth. We are a species that needs and wants to understand who we are.*
>
> —Anne Lamott

We're not going to write "A Vision" in this book (that would be two books in one). But we are going to show you how we started that story, by researching, taking notes, creating a topic sentence and synopsis, and developing characters, events, and locations for the action. Not surprisingly, these basic story components are also the components that WriteItNow provides for you to create your story. Apply our examples of how to use these components to your own stories. And write.

You can use the tools we discuss in this section at any stage of your writing. We present them in a logical order that you might use them in, but use them in any order. WriteItNow was designed to suit *your* personal writing style.

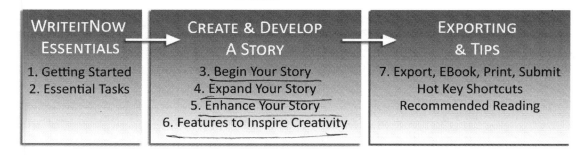

WriteItNow Essentials	Create & Develop a Story	Exporting & Tips
1. Getting Started 2. Essential Tasks	3. Begin Your Story 4. Expand Your Story 5. Enhance Your Story 6. Features to Inspire Creativity	7. Export, EBook, Print, Submit Hot Key Shortcuts Recommended Reading

Figure 1.1 Making the Most of WriteItNow 4 book structure.

In the last section (Chapter 7), we arrive at the *grand finale*: preparing your book for print!

Why WriteItNow?

WriteItNow is powerful and affordable. It allows you to Customize, Organize, Visualize, and Realize your writing adventure.

Why use writing software at all? Outlining scenes with pen and paper works and has worked well for centuries. Many great writers wrote before typewriters were in common use. And even today, some writers prefer to sit quietly at a desk without a computer.

But eventually, almost all modern writers will need to get their stories into printable format. That means getting them into a computer. If you're the kind of writer that organizes, plots, and writes without revision and needs only pen or pencil notes, then you might think you don't need some of WriteItNow's features. Yet.

We also write with pen and paper, and usually we begin our stories that way, by jotting notes and ideas and sketching out scenes in our notebooks. If you're like us, you'll find that WriteItNow can simplify your note taking and help you organize those preliminary ideas. After all, some of our first thoughts and inspirations are the ones worth pursuing. Once you've started writing your scenes in detail, WriteItNow shines as your writing assistant. For example, changing your mind about the location of a chapter or scene is simply a matter of dragging and dropping the chapter or scene to a new location.

WriteItNow is both a text or word processor as well as your story manager. If you're someone who has always wanted to write a story but couldn't make yourself write in a conventional word processor such as Word, then WriteItNow, is an excellent alternative. If you want to write, WriteItNow will help you write.

WriteItNow Software & Updates

WriteItNow was created by the good folks at Ravenshead Services in Scotland. The software is compatible with PCs (Windows 7, Vista, and XP) and Mac OSX. You can download the software or purchase a CD. To test whether this is the right writing software for you, download a free trial version of WriteItNow at the Ravenshead Services website:

www.ravensheadservices.com

If you have an older registered version (*e.g.,* WriteItNow 3), you can upgrade to WriteItNow 4 for a small fee at the Ravenshead website.

If you purchase a download version of WriteItNow 4, Ravenshead Services will email you the unlock codes to activate your copy. These codes convert the trial demonstration versions to fully registered versions of WriteItNow 4, which can save and use WriteItNow's special features, such as Add-Ons.

If you prefer a "hard copy" (*i.e.*, a WriteItNow CD), you can purchase it at Amazon (www.amazon.com), Pinyon Publishing (www.pinyon-publishing.com), or Ravenshead Services (www.ravensheadservices.com).

Ravenshead Services continually adds prompts, appearance options, name sets, background add-ons, and databases (for personality generators, appearance generators, and timelines). To check for feature updates, from WriteItNow's main menu, select File > Downloads and choose the type of update you're looking for. (Figure 1.2).

WriteItNow revisions are summarized at www.ravensheadservices.com/revisions.php.

Updates

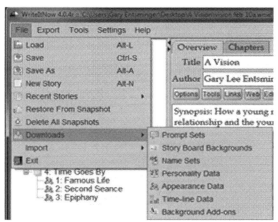

Figure 1.2 WriteItNow feature updates.

Updates

WHY WRITEITNOW?

CUSTOMIZE—Customize WriteItNow's display to work best for you. Show as many story components as you need. Show and hide views. Change fonts. Change your mind. No problem.

ORGANIZE—Organize the details and information about the characters and events in your story. Easily access that information, no matter where you are in your writing. Your initial notes are as accessible as your most recently inspired chapters and scenes. Moving scenes from one chapter to another is simply drag and drop. Moving a scene into your story from another program is simply cut and paste or through a menu-driven text or file import.

VISUALIZE—Use the Story Board to see your story as if it were a set of note cards laid out on a table. Your story comes alive card by card. You can shuffle and move them around. You can also view and rearrange your story with Tree View. Visualize character relationships and events with Graph features. Sometimes this visual take on your story's structure can help you see where your story needs to go.

REALIZE—When your story is ready to be shared with others, you have numerous formatting and export options.

WRITEITNOW SOFTWARE & UPDATES

CHAPTER 2
Essential Tasks

> *When you write, you lay out a line of words. The line of words is a miner's pick, a woodcarver's gouge, a surgeon's probe. You wield it, and it digs a path you follow. Soon you find yourself deep in new territory. Is it a dead end, or have you located the real subject? You will know tomorrow, or this time next year.*
>
> —*Annie Dillard*

The WriteItNow Main menu is your starting point for creating and loading new projects (Figure 2.1). Think of it as the primary access to your writing projects. It's where you save and export files, access tools (*e.g.,* the Story Board), customize the look and feel of WriteItNow, download the latest prompt sets, and access help.

For keyboard specialists (you know who you are), some menu items have hot key shortcuts. See page 106 for a complete list of WriteItNow keyboard shortcuts.

Create & Save a Story

In the beginning,

Create a new story file by selecting File > New Story (or Alt-N). Next, fill in the Title and Author text boxes (Figure 2.1).

WriteItNow gives every new story the default name "blank.wnw." The first time you save your story we suggest you give it a more meaningful name. From the Main menu, select File > Save As, and name your file.

Get in the habit of saving your story at timely intervals. We know writers and programmers who would regret losing ten minutes of their

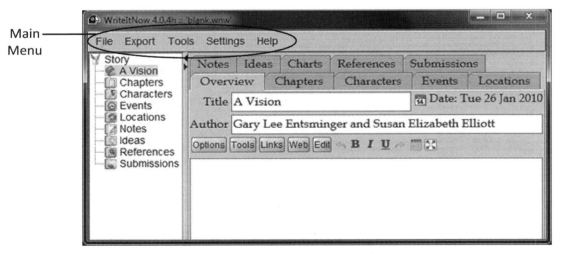

Main Menu

Figure 2.1 Create a Story: File > New Story. Fill in Title and Author.

hard-earned work. Can you afford to?

To save your story manually, select File > Save (or Ctrl-S). A window will pop up to tell you your file has been saved (under the current file name). If you want to save as a new name, select File > Save As (or Alt-A). A Save dialog opens (Figure 2.2). We suggest you create a new folder for each of your stories. Your story will be saved as a WriteItNow Story = .wnw file extension. You can also tell WriteItNow to save your story automatically at designated time intervals (see page 16).

Each time you close your document (even if you recently saved it), WriteItNow will ask if you want to save your story. It might sound redundant, but it could save you a good day's writing.

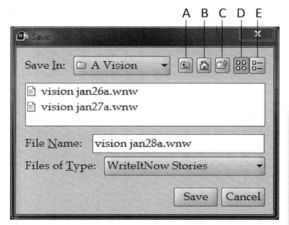

Figure 2.2 Save As: new story file name. File > Save As. **A.** Navigate up one level, **B.** Navigate to desktop, **C.** Create new folder, **D.** List items in folder, **E.** Detail list in folder.

SAVING TIPS

- Note that your operating system will date the file for you, but you should also consider adding your own date code to the file name.

- For example, each time we make a significant number of changes to a story, we update the name to reflect when during the day we made the change. In a day where we make a lot of changes to a document, we may save the file three times (*e.g.,* as vision jan26a.wnw, vision jan26b.wnw, and vision jan26c.wnw). This way, if we regret a change we made later in the day, we can easily find an earlier version.

- Fortunately, WriteItNow files (.wnw) are small, so you can save numerous copies without filling up your hard drive.

- Back up your work regularly to an external hard drive or flash drive. If your computer crashes, you still have all the versions of your story.

Zest. Gusto. How rarely one hears these words used. How rarely do we see people living, or for that matter, creating by them. Yet if I were asked to name the most important items in a writer's make-up, the things that shape his material and rush him along the road to where he wants to go, I could only warn him to look to his zest, see to his gusto.

—Ray Bradbury

Auto-Save & Snapshots

You can save your story manually to a .wnw file (using File > Save), or WriteItNow can automatically create backup files and save your work in the background while you're writing. These back up files (or "snapshots") can restore your story if something gets lost or corrupted.

You can also use back up files to retract those changes you made and now regret. Every time you Save normally (using File > Save), WriteItNow saves a .bak file as well as a .wnw file. In short, WriteItNow does everything it can to preserve your work.

You can tell WriteItNow how often to backup your files. Each backup file is called a snapshot because it's essentially a complete picture of your .wnw file at one instant in time. You can tell WriteItNow how many snapshots to keep. For example, if you ask WriteItNow to save snapshots every ten minutes and to keep three snapshots, then after you've been working for 40 minutes, WriteItNow will discard the earliest snapshot and keep the three most recent snapshots that were saved 20, 30, and 40 minutes after you began working.

To choose your Auto-Save settings, select Settings > Tool Settings > Auto-save and Snapshots (Figure 2.3).

To recover a file from a snapshot file (.bak), see Recovering a Story from a Snapshot (page 29).

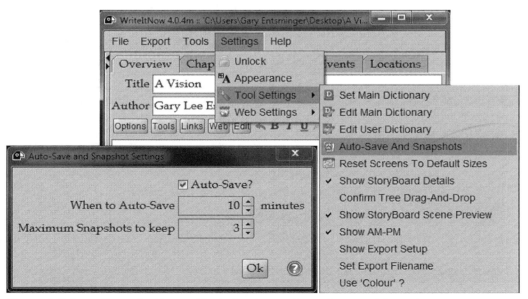

Figure 2.3 Auto-Save. Settings > Tools Settings > Auto-Save and Snapshots.

Customize the User Interface

The Appearance menu (Settings > Appearance) allows you to customize the WriteItNow interface. For example, you might want to show more or fewer tabs. To change the appearance of the tabs, select Settings > Appearance. The Appearance Settings window has three tabs (Look and Feel, Fonts, and Tabs). Select Tabs (Figure 2.4).

The Tabs tab shows you the organizational WriteItNow components (Overview, Chapters, Scenes, Characters, Events, Locations, Notes, Ideas, Graphs, References, and Submissions). You can display any or all of these by checking or unchecking the Visible check box (Figure 2.4).

By default, all WriteItNow components are checked. But suppose you prefer a simpler interface. You might not want to see components you don't intend to use just yet. For the example story in this book, "A Vision," it's a little early for References and Submissions, so to streamline our working area, let's uncheck those tabs (Figure 2.4).

When you return to your story, you no longer see the References or the Submissions tabs (Figure 2.4). Note also that you don't see them in Tree View either. Tree View and Tab View will always be synchronized with each other except for the Graphs tab, which does not appear in Tree View. Think of Tab View and Tree View as two ways to organize the same components in your story. Plus, you do your writing in the Tab View editor windows.

You can also rename tabs. For example, you may want to think of chapters as acts, characters as people, or locations as towns. If so, just relabel those components (see pages 32-34).

USER INTERFACE

A user interface (or UI) is the display that allows you to interact with a software program. This user interface is highly customizable in WriteItNow.

THE 10 COMPONENTS

Throughout this book we refer to WriteItNow "components." These are the ten writing structures or parts you work with while writing your story:

Chapters	Scenes
Characters	Events
Locations	Notes
Ideas	Graphs
References	Submissions

These also represent, we think, the main elements that compose most stories.

Ideas/Notes   Images (?)

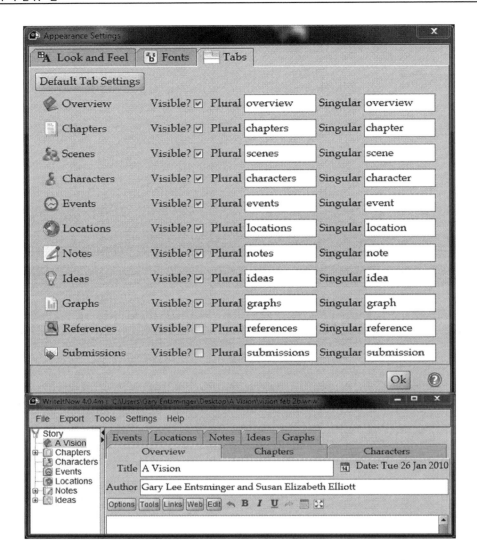

Figure 2.4 Customize Tabs Appearance dialog window and resulting interface.

In my experience, the pupil who sets down the night's dream, or recasts the day before into ideal form, who takes the morning hour to write a complete anecdote or a passage of sharp dialog, is likely to be the short story writer in embryo.

—*Dorethea Brande*

CUSTOMIZE THE USER INTERFACE

Tree View

There are two main ways to navigate through your story: Tree View and Tab View. Tree View is primarily an organizational view. It's on the left side of the WriteItNow display. Think of it as an outline of your story. For example, Figure 2.5 shows the outline of "Making the Most Of WriteItNow," which we wrote in WriteItNow. (Yes, you can write non-fiction in WriteItNow too!)

In Tree View you can view as many or as few of your story components as you want by clicking on the ⊞ and ⊟ buttons to the left of each component.

As your story becomes more complex, Tree View becomes invaluable. Use it to move scenes between chapters and to organize events, locations, characters, ideas, and notes. To move a scene within a chapter or to a different chapter, drag and drop. You can also change the order of other story components (characters, ideas, locations, and so on) within their respective sections with a simple drag and drop.

WRITEITNOW HELP

Many WriteItNow features have a blue question mark in their pop-up windows. Click on the question mark to learn more about the feature.

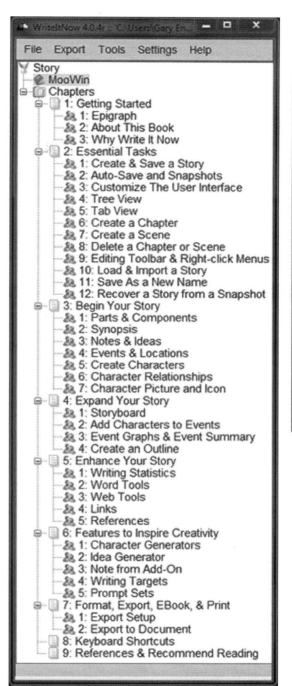

Figure 2.5 Tree view.

Tab View

Tab View is the right side of the WriteItNow display. Tab View is useful for navigating through your story, but more important, it's where you'll write your story.

Each tab contains its own navigational toolbar, editing toolbar, and editor window (Figure 2.6). The navigational toolbar lets you move forward and backward to other entries (*e.g.*, characters, chapters, scenes, or events).

The ➕ and ➖ buttons in the navigational toolbar allow you to add or delete entries. See Editing Toolbar & Right-click Menus (page 23) to learn how to use the editing toolbar.

The Characters tab contains an editor window where you describe and develop your characters. The Overview tab contains an editor window and tools for you to summarize your story. The Overview tab has no navigational toolbar because you need only one entry for your overview.

The Graphs tab has two sub-tabs with unique toolbars which we explain in Chapter 4 (page 52). The Chapters tab has sub-tabs for chapter details and scenes. The Chapter Details

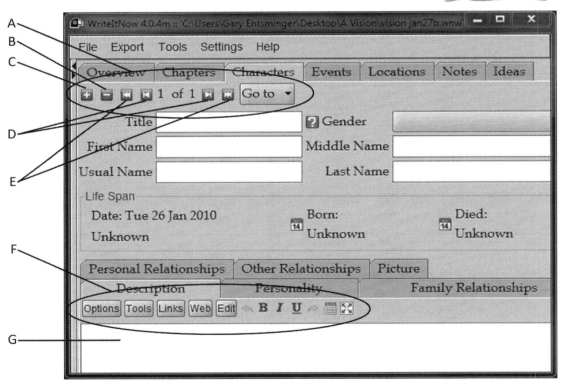

Figure 2.6 Tab View. **A.** Navigational toolbar, **B.** Delete, **C.** Add, **D.** Go back/forward one, **E.** Go back/forward to first/last, **F.** Editing toolbar, **G.** Editor window.

sub-tab is a good place to record general notes or a synopsis of the chapter. Write the bulk of your story in the Scene Editor sub-tab.

Notice the two navigational toolbars on the Chapters tab. The upper navigational toolbar moves you through chapters (Figure 2.7A), while the lower one moves you through scenes within the selected chapter (Figure 2.7B).

TREE & TAB VIEW

Use the two arrows on the edge between the Tree and Tab View to open or close either view. Resize the Tree View by clicking anywhere along that edge and dragging the Tree View smaller or larger. To resize the Tab View, click on the right edge of WriteItNow and drag the Tab View smaller or larger.

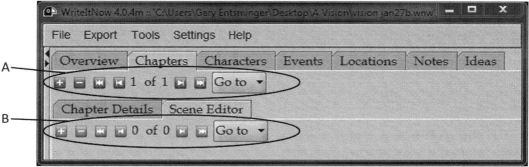

Figure 2.7 Chapter (*A*) and Scene (*B*) navigational toolbars.

Create a Chapter

So you've given your story a name and saved it to a file. What next? That depends—on you and how much you know about your story. If you prefer to think simply, scene by scene and chapter by chapter, like Dickens and Tolstoy, WriteItNow provides the tools. If you've already written scenes and chapters in another program, you can import them into your story (see page 25).

WriteItNow is flexible and doesn't force anyone to write in any specific way. If you don't have a preferred method of operation, we suggest a simple approach: store all of your story text within chapters and scenes, and store your research and background information in notes and ideas.

To create chapters and scenes, use Tab View on the right side of the window. Select Chapter and click the button in the navigational toolbar (Figure 2.8A). Name your chapter.

Chapter/Scenes

Create a Scene

Although you don't have to use scenes in your story, we recommend it. By breaking your story into parts, you make your story more manageable. Most stories have underlying scenes where separate events (*e.g.*, conversations, murders, seductions) occur.

To create a new scene, select the Chapters tab. Within a chapter (add one if you haven't already), select the Scene Editor sub-tab. Select the ⊞ button on the scene navigational toolbar. Give your scene a name in the Title box, and you're good to go (Figure 2.9).

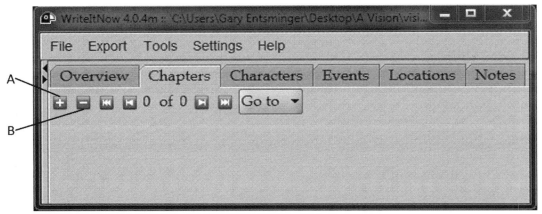

Figure 2.8 Create chapter. **A.** Add new chapter, **B.** Delete an existing chapter.

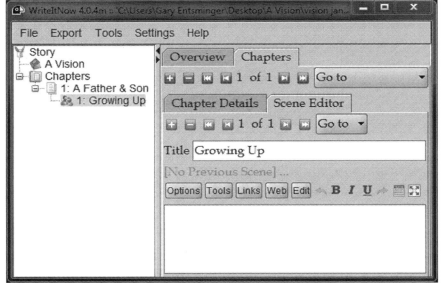

Figure 2.9 Create a scene.

Delete a Chapter or Scene

To delete a chapter, scene, or any other component, click the ▣ button in the navigational toolbar just below the tab (Figure 2.8B). If this entry contains typing, WriteItNow will ask you if you're sure you want to delete it. This reminder makes it harder for you to accidently delete information.

Editing Toolbar & Right-click Menus

Each editor window has a dedicated editing toolbar. For example, the scene editor, like the chapter details editor, has a toolbar containing a row of buttons between the Title box and the editor window (Figure 2.9). You can also access these tools (except "Options") with a right-click in the editor window (Figure 2.10).

The Graphs tab has a menu bar for printing and other tasks specific to graphs (Figure 2.11) Use the toolbars and menus for quick access to many useful functions. Later in this book (Chapter 5: Enhance Your Story, page 56), we'll demonstrate other useful features you can access from the editing toolbar.

> *First thoughts have tremendous energy. It is the way the mind flashes on something. The internal censor usually squelches them, so we live in the realm of second and third thoughts, thoughts on thought, twice and three times removed from the direct connection of the first fresh flash.*
>
> —*Natalie Goldberg*

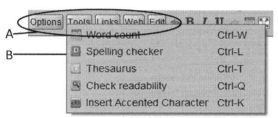

Figure 2.10 Editing toolbar (*A*) and right-click pop-up menu (*B*).

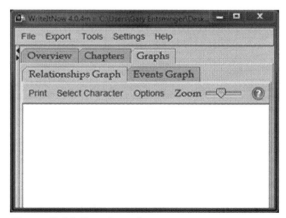

Figure 2.11 Graphs tab.

> *What the beginning writer ordinarily wants is a set of rules on what to do and what not to do in writing fiction. As we'll see, some general principles can be set down and some general warnings can be offered; but on the whole the search for aesthetic absolutes is a misapplication of the writer's energy.*
>
> —John Gardner

Load a WriteItNow Story

Suppose you began a story and then closed WriteItNow. How do you reopen your story? WriteItNow keeps track of the previous nine stories you worked on. Each time WriteItNow opens, it loads the most recent of these stories. So if that's the one you want, you've got it. No work needed. Just open WriteItNow and your most recent story will automatically load.

To load another recent story, select File > Recent Stories > Load. Then select the story you want to Load (Figure 2.12). You can also clear the list of recently loaded stories by selecting File > Recent Stories > Clear All. This does not delete the stories; it just removes them from the list.

To Load a story that is not in your recent story list, select File > Load from the Main menu. A dialog window opens to the current folder (Figure 2.13). Select a file from that folder or navigate to a new folder.

CREATE A TITLE

If you're starting a new story, use the Create Title option on the Overview tab for ideas.

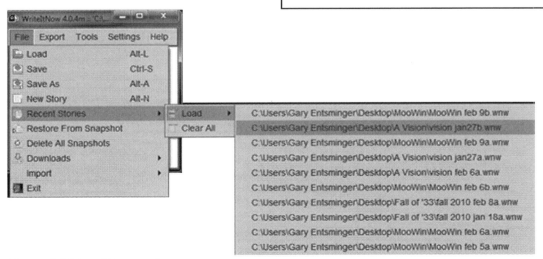

Figure 2.12 Load Recent Story.

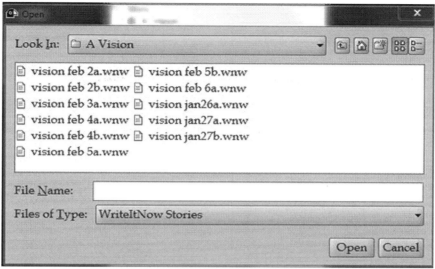

Figure 2.13 File Load dialog.

Import a non-WriteItNow File

You can import text from other programs using File > Import. WriteItNow can import .rtf (Rich Text Format) files. Many word processors, such as Microsoft Word, can create .rtf files. To create an .rtf file in Word, for example, when you select Save As, choose Rich Text Format as the file type from the drop down menu (Figure 2.14).

Rich text files retain most, if not all, of the word processor's formatting. However, when you import an .rtf into WriteItNow, all of this formatting may not be retained. For example, WriteItNow uses underlines to designate chapters. So any underlined words in your text will start a new WriteItNow chapter. Bold and italic .rtf formatting will not be conserved in WriteItNow.

You can work on aspects of a story in WriteItNow (your chapters and scenes text), then export to Word (exporting is covered in Chapter 7, page 96) to get a preview of how it will look when it's formatted for a printer or publisher. If you make formatting changes in Word, your story may not import back into WriteItNow the way you expect it to.

Thus, it's best to think of .rtf importing and exporting as primarily one-way processes: either (1) importing documents you haven't worked on in WriteItNow before or (2) exporting documents that you don't intend to import back into WriteItNow.

Figure 2.14 Save As an .rtf file in Word.

If you want to import text into a story you're currently working on in WriteItNow, select File > Import > RTF from the Main menu (Figure 2.15). Note that the imported file will be added to your current story if the story is open.

To create a completely new story from an .rtf file of previous work, first create a new (blank) story in WriteItNow, then import the .rtf file. For example, Figure 2.16A shows you what it would look like if the .rtf file you imported had one chapter.

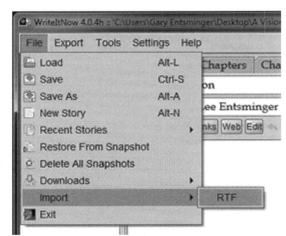

Figure 2.15 Import .rtf navigation.

Now suppose you have a second .rtf that contains another chapter. Keep your current story open, then import the second .rtf file (Figure 2.16B). If you've already written a chunk of your story in another word processor, you'll find this importing tool useful. As you can see, you can have more control over the import if you start by separating your previous work into chapters or sections and saving each section as a separate .rtf file.

Arguably, the easiest way to import plain text is to Copy and Paste. If you're unsure about importing .rtf(s), but you've already written a chunk of your story in another program, such as Word, follow these steps:

1. Create a new story.

2. Create a blank chapter or scene for each chapter or scene in your manuscript. For example, go to the Chapters tab and click on the ⊞ button for each chapter.

3. To manually import each chapter or scene individually, first load your text into a word processor. Select the entire text of a chapter or scene. Copy it to the clipboard (Ctrl+C on PCs or CMD+C on Macs).

4. Go to the new blank WriteItNow chapter. Paste the text to the blank chapter or scene (Ctrl+V on PCs or CMD+V on Macs).

5. Repeat for each chapter or scene.

6. Save.

Another alternative is to save the text to import as a plain text file. Then within any tab editor window, place the cursor where the text is to be imported. Click Edit > Import Plain Text File (Figure 2.17).

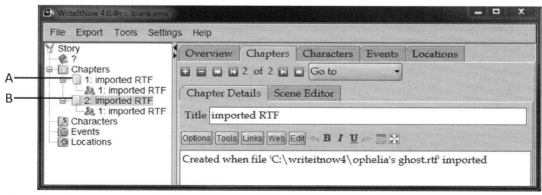

A—
B—

Figure 2.16 Import two .rtfs (*A* and *B*).

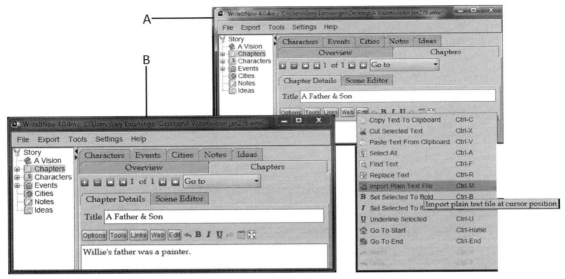

Figure 2.17 Import plain text menu (*A*) and result (*B*).

Save As a New Name

If you've checked Auto Save (in Settings > Tool Settings), then WriteItNow will save backups files (.bak) at the intervals you selected (see page 16). At any time, use File > Save (Ctrl-S) to save the current story as a WriteItNow file (.wnw).

To save your story to a new file name, from the Main menu select File > Save As. The File Save dialog window opens. Type in a new name (Figure 2.18).

The current story will be updated with the new name. But note that the old version of the story still exists, and you can Load it at any time. The old version will also appear in your recent stories list from the Main menu, File > Recent Stories > Load.

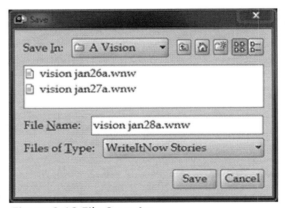

Figure 2.18 File Save As.

SAVE STORY NAME

Save your stories with the same file name as the story title. This makes them easy to find.

SAVE AS A NEW NAME

Recovering a Story from a Snapshot

To recover a previous version of your story that was automatically saved as a snapshot (.bak file), in the Main menu, select File > Restore From Snapshot (Figure 2.19A).

The Restore Snapshot dialog window opens to show you the current saved snapshots (Figure 2.19B). Click OK, and WriteItNow displays a warning to remind you of what you're about to do (Figure 2.19C).

As a precaution, save the current story before restoring from a snapshot. If you don't like the snapshot, you can then restore it from the saved story file.

Vigorous writing is concise. A sentence should contain no unnecessary words, a paragraph no unnecessary sentences, for the same reason that a drawing should have no unnecessary lines and a machine no unnecessary parts.

—William Strunk Jr. and E.B. White

CLEAN UP

To clear out old back-up files use the Delete All Snapshots option on the File menu.

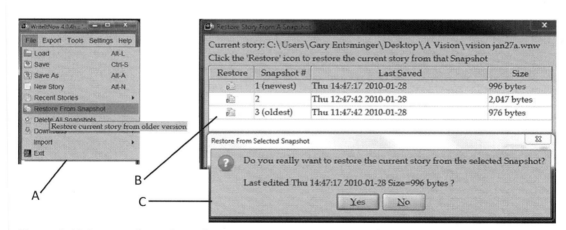

Figure 2.19 Restore from Snapshot. **A.** Menu, **B.** Pop-up window, **C.** Warning.

CREATE & DEVELOP A STORY

CHAPTER 3 Begin Your Story

> *On his way to the garden gate, the writer suddenly turned around. He rushed into the house and up to his study and substituted one word for another. It was only then that he smelled the sweat in the room and saw the mist on the windowpanes.*
>
> —Peter Handke

Parts & Components

Suppose you're writing your first story, and you don't know everything about it when you start. You have a beginning, an ending, and maybe some stops along the way. For example, a son is frustrated with his father's advice to stay the course, and he's determined to make his own decisions. Their relationship becomes strained, which creates new problems for both of them. Later, an unexpected discovery enables the son to understand why his father gave the advice.

Or perhaps your thoughts aren't even that organized; you just have some notes or a few ideas. WriteItNow can help by: (1) giving you the tools to organize what you do know and (2) letting you separate different aspects of your story into easily recognizable components (*e.g.*, events, locations, notes, and ideas). These components provide a place to store information about your story in easily retrievable and identifiable chunks.

For example, most stories consist of *characters* that you put in places (or *locations*). They participate in *events* that move the story along. If your story occurs in several cities, like an episode of "Alias," you might want to list those cities (*i.e.*, locations) and information about them so that you can easily find them later. Similarly, if events occur in these places at particular times, you can use WriteItNow to link the events to specific characters and locations.

Writing your story was probably preceded by considerable imagination and research. WriteItNow lets you easily add notes at any time to store those gems and link them to other components (*e.g.*, scenes). We'll show you examples of how to do this on page 73. For now, simply click the Link button in the editing toolbar in Tab View (or right-click in the editor window). This shows you at a glance the components available (Figure 3.1). Use this menu to add links to any available component.

Notice also that we've been using "places" and "locations" interchangeably. But we also said that a story's places could be "cities" or "location sets" if you're writing a screenplay. (Yes, you can use WriteItNow to write a screenplay!) If you want a clearer picture of the names of components in the WriteItNow Tree and Tab Views, then customize your display to reflect your name preferences.

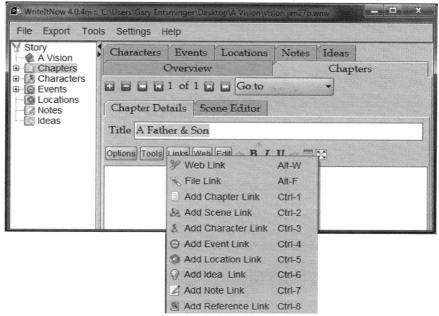

Figure 3.1 Link Menu.

What, then, are the essential problems of depicting consciousness in fiction? There are two orders of them and both come from the nature of consciousness itself. First, a particular consciousness, we assume, is a private thing; and second, consciousness is never static but is always in a state of motion.

—Robert Humphrey

To change the name of a tab, from the Main menu, select Settings > Appearance. Then select the Tabs tab. Change tab names in the appropriate text boxes. When you return to the story, you'll see the new name (*e.g.,* cities instead of locations) in both Tab and Tree Views (Figure 3.2).

The Notes tab is useful for making notes about your story. No doubt, you'll be inspired by some occurrence or thought that you need to jot down immediately before you lose it. Or perhaps you come upon a piece of information that you'd like to use somewhere in your story, but you're not sure where. Create a note for it.

Later, cut and paste the note (or a modified version of the note) into the chapter or scene where you want to use it. The edit menu on the editing toolbar above the editor window contains numerous features for moving text into or around your story (Figure 3.3).

You can also import text from a file into a component (*e.g.,* a note or scene) by selecting Edit > Import Plain text. A file dialog window opens (Figure 3.4). Other components behave similarly, although each component has its own special features. We'll detail these features using examples throughout this book.

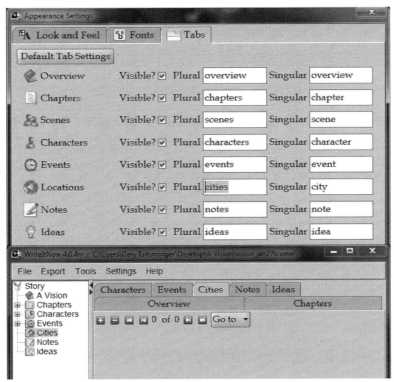

Figure 3.2 Customize Tab View.

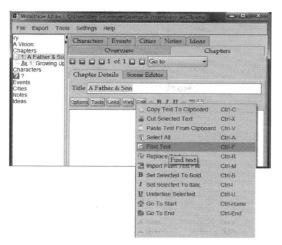

Figure 3.3 Edit Menu.

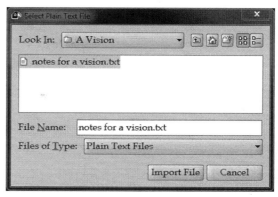

Figure 3.4 Import Plain Text.

Synopsis

There are as many ways to write as there are writers. And many writers have written books about writing and the writing life (see Recommended Reading, page 107). In this book, we won't try to teach you how to write. Instead, we'll show you how to use WriteItNow to organize your story and keep it moving forward.

Earlier we showed you the first step toward writing a story in WriteItNow: create and save your story to a file. When you create a story, you name it. That sounds trivial perhaps, but the title of your story is the first step, and each step in your story is important. Your title helps you focus on your story's overall meaning and your goals for the story.

If you're a beginning writer or a writer without a plan, we suggest you begin by writing a sentence about your story. You might think of this as your response when someone asks, "What's the story about?" Or the sentence can be the idea behind your story, the premise, or perhaps what inspired you to write this story. It need not be polished or complete, and it's very unlikely this sentence will ever appear in your story.

Write your sentence or synopsis in the Overview editor (Figure 3.5). You can get to the Overview editor using Tab View or Tree View. Take as long as you need to write it. Then take a deep breath and write another sentence about your story, and another, until you've written a paragraph (Figure 3.6).

You might think of this paragraph as the synopsis of your story. What you choose to write is of course specific to your story and will vary in

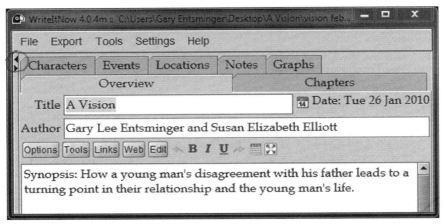

Figure 3.5 Synopsis sentence.

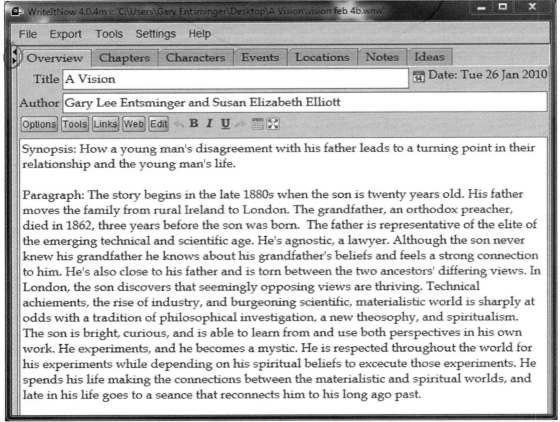

Figure 3.6 Synopsis paragraph.

structure from story to story. For example, you might write a paragraph summing up the plot or a paragraph indicating that the story is about a character's emotional development. Whatever works for you works, but try to get some of your enthusiasm about wanting to write your story in the paragraph.

Writing this synopsis paragraph should not feel intimidating. Think of it as an exercise to develop clarity, a short meditation, or an overview of your story. It's the place where you remind yourself of what your story is about. It's also a place where you get your fingers typing and your mind rolling. Return to this paragraph and revise it as your story evolves.

We've closed Tree View in Figure 3.6. Recall that you use the two arrows on the border of Tree and Tab Views to open or close either view.

Notes & Ideas

Suppose you have an idea or a note to record for your story. WriteItNow gives you two dedicated components to use: Notes and Ideas.

We'll define a note as an annotation, a brief record or list of facts, a reminder, or anything else that might be useful to your story. For example, "The Theosophical Society was founded by Helena Blavatsky in 1875 to advance spiritual principles and to search for truth."

In contrast, we'll define an idea as being something more specific to your story, a thought, a suggestion, or a possible course of action. For example, "Defiant, the son goes to his first seance in London."

When you use the Idea Generator and Note Add-Ons (pages 83-86), you'll see this distinction more clearly.

Notes and ideas are useful as "scratch pads." You can make notes and record ideas while keeping your story's main writing area (chapters and scenes) uncluttered. When a note or idea looks useful enough, you can copy and paste the parts you need into your scene. Or you can just use the note or idea for inspiration.

To create a note, select Note in Tree or Tab View. In Tab View, click the ⊞ button. Create a title for your note and type the idea in the editor window (Figure 3.7). You can also create a note from an Add-On (page 85).

Similarly, to create an idea, select Idea in Tree or Tab View. In Tab View, click the ⊞ button. Create a title for your idea and type the idea in the editor window (Figure 3.7).

NOTES & IDEAS

Think of notes as brief comments, lists of facts, and reminders. Think of ideas as thoughts that are more specific to your story.

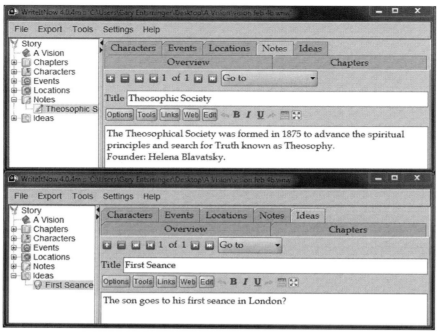

Figure 3.7 Create Note (*Above*) and Idea (*Below*).

Events & Locations

At this point, you're at a crossroads. You've defined your story, but nothing has happened yet. There are no characters and no places for events to occur. What next?

Here's another opportunity for you to be creative and develop your own writing style. For example, if you think your story is primarily about character development, then create your characters next. If your story hinges on an event, such as a presidential debate or a tragedy, then you might want to establish the event first. If your story focuses on place, such as the deep south of a Faulkner novel, then you might want to create your place first. You're the director, and WriteItNow leaves all possibilities open.

In our example story, "A Vision," a young father moves his family from rural Ireland to London. Later (in an undisclosed location) he attends a seance. That's two places and one event to start. Or say we realize that two seances (one early and one late in the young man's life) would create nice symmetry. So that's two events; let's create them first.

To create an event, select Event in Tree or Tab View. In Tab View, click the button. Create a title for your event and type the event details in the editor window (Figure 3.8).

In Figure 3.8 notice the middle pane beside

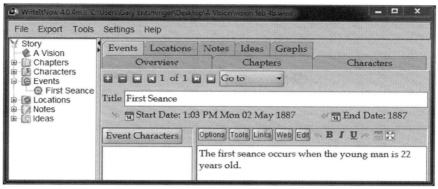

Figure 3.8 Create event.

the editor window with the Event Character button. If you've created characters, you can add characters to the event here (see page 52). This might make you think you should always create characters before you create an event. But WriteItNow again shows its flexibility. You can add characters to an event anytime. (You can also remove characters from an event anytime.)

Let's also say that the first seance will take place in London and the second in Dublin. That's three places: (1) rural Ireland, say Drumcliff, (2) London, and (3) Dublin. So let's create those locations.

To create a location, select Location in Tree or Tab View. In Tab View, click the button. Create a title for your location and type the location details in the editor window. Repeat for the other locations (Figure 3.9)

Use Tree View to review all the components you've added to your story (Figure 3.10).

EVENTS & LOCATIONS

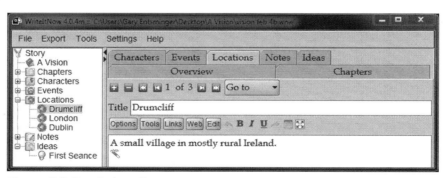

Figure 3.9 Create location.

Figure 3.10 Use Tree View to visualize all the story components you've added to your story.

Of "War and Peace" it has never been suggested, I suppose, that Tolstoy here produced a model of perfect form. It is a panoramic vision of people and places, a huge expanse in which armies are marshalled; can one expect of such a book that it should be neatly composed?

—Percy Lubbock

Create Characters

Let's get some characters into the story. Since, in our example story, we're developing the consequences of a conflict between a father and his son, we need to know more about the father and his son. What is the father's occupation? (He's a barrister and painter.) Is he religious? (No. He's agnostic.) Always agnostic? (No, his father had been a Rector in the Church of Ireland.) Was the son also agnostic? (No, his religious or spiritual beliefs fell somewhere in-between his father and grandfather.) And so on. We also might want to know who attends the two seances. Did the participants know each other before the seance? Or are they meeting for the first time? And if so, how have they happened to this same place now?

If you have a great memory, you needn't bother writing down these details. If not, let WriteItNow help you remember who's who.

To create a character, select the Characters tab. Then click the ⊞ button. Name your character and designate his or her gender (Figure 3.11).

To set the character's birthday (or death date, if applicable), select the calendar 🗓 button next to Born or Died. Change the year and select the date. Specify how much date information you want WriteItNow to display (month, day of month, day of week, BC) (Figure 3.12).

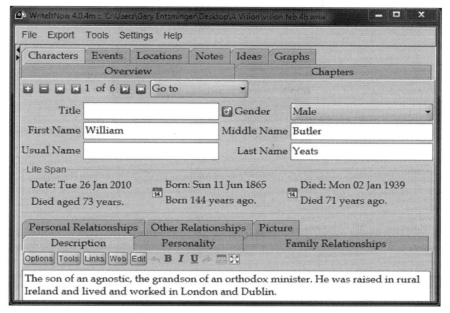

Figure 3.11 Create a character.

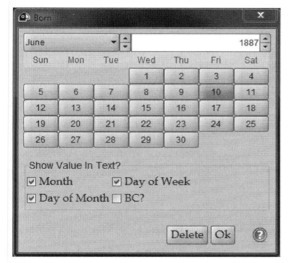

Figure 3.12 Calendar pop-up window.

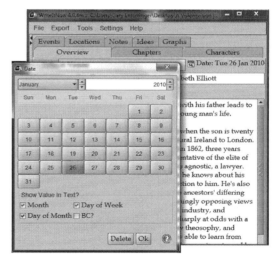

Figure 3.13 Set Story date.

Note that the story date is undefined, so in Figure 3.11 our Date reads "Tue 26 Jan 2010," the current date. To change your story date, go to the Overview tab, click the calendar 🗓 button to the right of your story title, and set the story date (Figure 3.13). Once WriteItNow has the story date information, it will display character ages at the current story date.

Back in the Character tab, within the Description sub-tab, describe the character in the editor window (Figure 3.14)

WriteItNow has special features to help you describe your character's personality in the Personality sub-tab. Instead of simply describing the personality in an editor window, go to the left panel of the Personality sub-tab. Click Add a Personality Trait and a choose a trait from the pop-up window drop-down (Figure 3.15). Click OK. This personality trait is added.

Suppose you chose the trait Affection. Click the value cell to adjust the sliding scale (default value = 50) to indicate that your character is strongly affectionate (high value) or strongly unaffectionate (low value) (Figure 3.15). For example, when the personality trait of wisdom set at a high value, this means the character is very wise. Wisdom set to a low value means the character is not wise. WriteItNow summarizes your character's personality traits in the Personality right panel (Figure 3.16). Move traits up and down by using the arrows in the left panel. The trait first in the list is designated as your character's most outstanding personality trait (Figure 3.16).

Create as many characters as your story needs, now or later, as you need them. Note that the information you use in your character descriptions and relationships need not occur in your story. You might even create background characters that influence other characters but do not actually appear in your story. Characters have histories, and most of the details of a

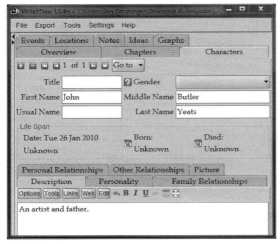

Figure 3.14 Descriptions tab.

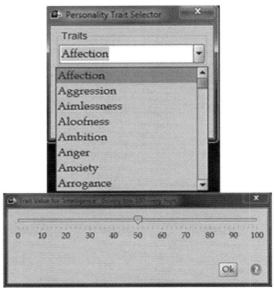

Figure 3.15 Personality trait selector (*Above*) and value scale (*Below*).

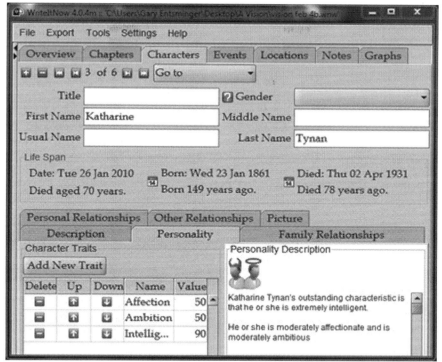

Figure 3.16 Personality overview.

character's life do not appear in the story. But the more you can imagine about the character, the easier it will be for you make his or her behavior believable in your story. If a character is married and unhappy or unemployed, that might explain why she's attracted to unreliable lovers. Use the Character Relationships tabs to help you flesh out these details.

The center of every Shakespearean play, as of all great literature, is character; and it is Hamlet's panic, rage, and indecisiveness that raises the question of what made him act so decisively this once—the question Shakespeare does not answer.

—John Gardner

Character Relationships

Now that we have some characters, let's imagine for a moment how these characters are related to each other. WriteItNow understands three types of relationships between characters: family, personal, and other.

Since William is related to his father, this is a family relationship. To create a family relationship, select the Family Relationships sub-tab. Add a relationship by clicking the button. A blank row appears. Click in any of the empty cells to open the dialog box (Figure 3.17).

In the dialog box, specify the type of relationship and the characters involved in the relationship. If applicable, use the calendar buttons to specify how long the relationship lasted. For example, let's specify that William Yeats is the "Son of" John Yeats (Figure 3.17).

Click OK, and WriteItNow adds the relationship. Delete relationships with the button (Figure 3.18). Reorder relationships with the arrow buttons.

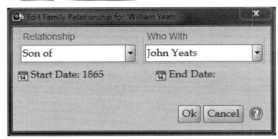

Figure 3.17 Family relationship.

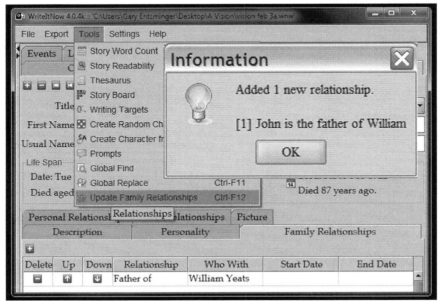

Figure 3.18 Update family relationship.

You can also make certain that new Relationships are reciprocal. For example, we've just noted that William is the son of John, and we want to note that therefore, John is the father of William. After adding family relationships, from the Main menu, select Tools > Update Relationships (or Ctrl-F12), and a window will pop up, showing you the reciprocal relationship that has been added (Figure 3.18).

Also, Katharine is a friend of William. This is a Personal relationship. William might have another type of relationship (*e.g.*, a professional relationship), which we can record in the Other Relationships sub-tab. Personal and Other Relationships are added the same way as Family Relationships. As with personality traits, you can specify the intensity of a personal relationship. For example, because Katharine is a very close friend of William, we'll indicate that by adjusting the sliding scale to Very Strong (Figure 3.19).

> *Writers work with words and voices just as painters work with colors; and where do these words and voices come from? Many sources: conversations heard and overheard, movies and radio broadcasts, newspapers and magazines, yes, and other writers; a phrase comes into the mind from an old western story in a pulp magazine read years ago, can't remember where or when: 'He looked at her, trying to read her mind—but her eyes were old, unbluffed, unreadable.' That's one that I lifted.*
>
> —William S. Burroughs

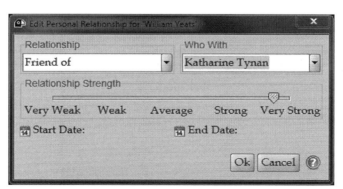

Figure 3.19 Relationship strength.

You can also view character relationships in a graph. If you need to, return to File > Settings > Appearance Tabs and check the Graphs tab box ("Charts" in older WriteItNow versions). Select the Graphs tab (Figure 3.20). Note that the Graphs feature is only in Tab View. It does not appear in Tree View.

The graph shows all the relationships (family, personal, and other) for a selected character. Change the focal character by clicking Select Character. You can also double-click on a character in the graph to make them the focal character.

You can move the characters around in the relationship graph to change your view. Under Options, you can customize the colors (coded by relationship type), numbers of levels (*e.g.,* do you want to show friends of friends or just "first order" friends?), spacing, and spread.

Character Picture & Icon

You can import a picture for each character. Pictures can be .png, .gif, or .jpg files. You should use small image files (< 100k and < 300 x 300 pixels). Large pictures aren't necessary and can slow WriteItNow response time. If you have a much bigger picture you want to use, then convert this to a smaller picture using a picture editing program (*e.g.,* Picassa or IrfanView).

To add a picture to a character, select a character, and then select the Picture sub-tab. Make sure the Image vertical sub-tab to the left is selected (Figure 3.21).

Click the New Picture button and navigate to your picture file. By default, the file selector shows previews of .png, .gif, and .jpg files.

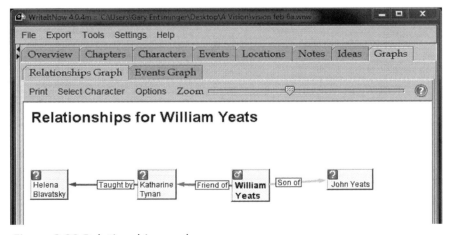

Figure 3.20 Relationship graph.

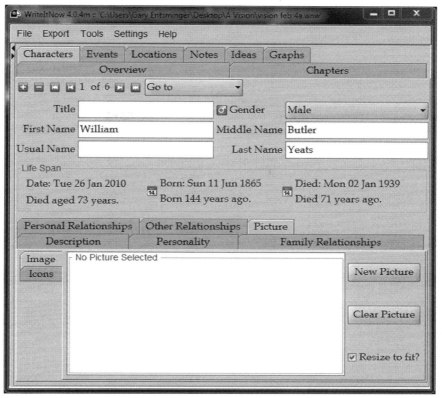

Figure 3.21 Picture tab.

Select your image file and click Select Image. Your new picture will appear in the viewing window (Figure 3.22). If you want WriteItNow to maximize the picture size in the viewing window, check the box for Resize to Fit. You may want to contemplate this picture as you are brainstorming certain aspects of your story.

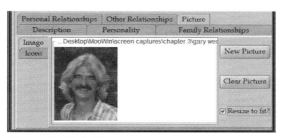

Figure 3.22 Add new picture.

You can create a character icon from the picture to replace the default gender symbol icon. The advantage of using pictures is that you can pick exactly which image to use for each character, and you can quickly go that character without reading the names. The disadvantage is that often pictures do not look good as icons. You will probably want to use full head shots for picture icons.

One solution is to use pictures that are the same size as the tree icons (16 x 16 dpi, 24 x 24 dpi, 32 x 32 dpi or 48 x 48 dpi). Note that picture resolution is usually given in dpi (dots per inch) or ppi (pixels per inch). Usually these units are interchangeable.

To set a picture as your character's icon, click the Icons vertical sub-tab on the left side of the Picture window, and click Make Icon from Image (Figure 3.23).

If you opt for a simple icon, you can customize the icon by clicking Use Simple Icon (from the icon sub-tab) or by clicking on the icon that appears next to the gender box. The Simple Icon Editor opens (Figure 3.24). A simple icon consists of three parts:

1. The rectangular background (which can be one of 12 colors).

2. The gender symbol for males, females, or unknown.

3. The symbol color (which can be any color from the Color Picker).

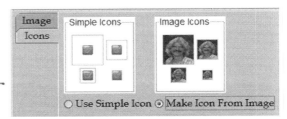

Figure 3.23 Make icon from image.

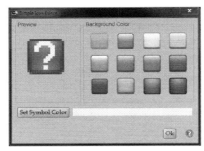

Figure 3.24 Simple icon editor.

ORGANIZE YOUR STORY: A BEGINNER'S JOURNEY

Premise/ Overview Write a sentence about your story. Think of this sentence as the concept behind your story, the premise, or perhaps the idea that inspired you to want to write this story.

Synopsis Write a paragraph that expands your overview sentence. Think of this paragraph as your synopsis, summary, or description of the main points of your story.

Setting/ Locations Where does your story take place? Remember a realtor's mantra—Location, location, location. Locations are where things happen, where your events occur. They also help you create the mood for your story.

Characters Almost any good story depends on carefully developed characters. Characters not only act (or live) in the story, but they lived before your story started, and their histories affect their behavior now. Imagine your character as fully as possible.

Actions/ Events These are the actions that propel your story. Even if your story is more concerned with character or a character's development than plot, actions are still crucial to the story. Something always happens, then something else happens.

Notes/ Ideas If you have an inspiration or idea, write it down. Don't worry if it's not a completely developed idea or if your note is simply a reminder to look something up. These inspirational gems can be very useful.

Prompts For more ideas like these to get your story started, check out WriteItNow's prompt sets (page 88).

CHARACTER PICTURE & ICON

CHAPTER 4 Expand Your Story

> *I write many thousands of words a day and some of them go on paper. And of those which are written down, only a few are ever meant to be seen.*
>
> —John Steinbeck

Story Board

As your story develops, add scenes, events, locations, notes, ideas, and characters as you need them. As your story becomes more complex, the more useful WriteItNow becomes, helping you stay organized.

One exceptional feature of WriteItNow is its Story Board. It displays your story's chapters and scenes in a different and very useful way. You might think of the Story Board as a board or table where you lay out your chapters and scenes like note cards. Some of our best writers (*e.g.,* Vladimir Nabokov and James Joyce) used note cards to write and reorganize their novels.

To load the Story Board, from the Main menu, select Tools > Story Board (or Ctrl-F5) (Figure 4.1). The Story Board opens, displaying the chapters and scenes in the story. You can now see your story as in a set of note cards, as if on a table (Figure 4.2).

Rearrange note cards (chapters and scenes) by dragging and dropping. WriteItNow will automatically keep track of the new order.

But the Story Board isn't just an organizer. It has its own editor as well, so you can edit a chapter or scene as a note card by double-clicking on the chapter or scene you want to edit. An editor window opens (Figure 4.3).

Notice that the Story Board editor has a full set of edit options available in the editing toolbar (or right-click for options) (Figure 4.4).

When you finish editing a chapter or scene, close the editor. The chapter or scene is automatically updated in the Story Board card. In turn, when you exit the Story Board, any changes to chapters or scenes are automatically updated in the appropriate Tab View editor(s).

You can also print your Story Board and change the settings of the Story Board (*e.g.,* background colors) from the Options menu (Figure 4.5).

Figure 4.1 Load Story Board.

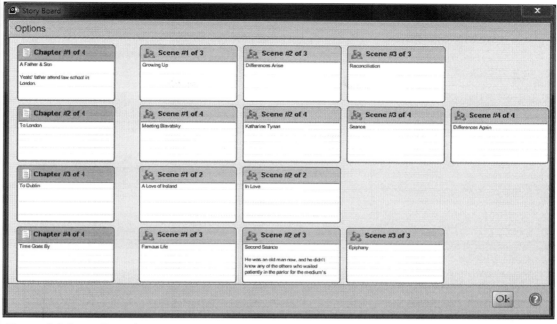

Figure 4.2 Story Board.

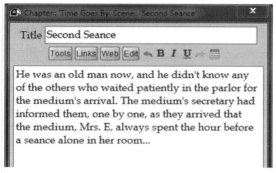

Figure 4.3 Story Board editor window.

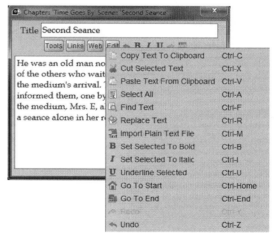

Figure 4.4 Story Board editor menu.

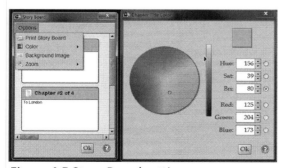

Figure 4.5 Story Board settings.

Add Characters to Events

Earlier we created an event. Now let's add characters to that event. Move to the Events tab and click the Event Characters button. A dialog window opens to show you all the characters in the story. Check the characters you want to add to the event (Figure 4.6).

Note that you can add and delete characters to an event anytime. Thus, as your story evolves, you can add characters and events as needed.

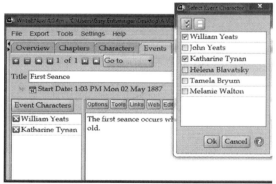

Figure 4.6 Add characters to event.

I came to write this book in order to find out whether I could articulate certain feelings that I had had since very early days with sufficient clarity, and justify them with sufficient force, as to make out of them a kind of incantation which should serve to drive away from other natures, kindred to my own, the particular demons that I have suffered from, throughout my long years of lecturing in the large cities of this country.

—John Cowper Powys

Event Graphs & Event Summary

To visualize your events, go to the Graphs tab and select the Events graph (Figure 4.7). The graph in the window color codes each event (Figure 4.7G). The length of the bar represents the duration of the event (defined when you add an event). In our sample story, we have two events displayed.

By default, the graph maximizes how much you can see in the graph. If however, you want to look at events over a shorter or longer time period, adjust the time scale above the graph (Figure 4.7H).

In the toolbar to the left of the sliding time scale are options to print the graph and change the graph background color (Figure 4.7C,D).

If you only want to see the events that certain characters are involved in, click the character button (Figure 4.7B) and de-select the characters you do not want (Figure 4.7I).

The event order buttons (Figure 4.7E), toggle the graph between showing events in chronological order or with the newer, more recent, events first (to the left).

To get an event summary (Figure 4.8), go to the Events tab, and click Options > Event Summary. Note that you can also print the event summary.

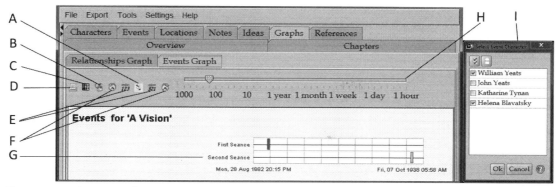

Figure 4.7 Events graph. **A.** Maximize display, **B.** Select event characters, **C.** Background color, **D.** Print, **E.** Sort (oldest-newest or newest to oldest), **F.** Display previous/next time period, **G.** Events timeline graph , **H.** Time range displayed, **I.** Select event characters.

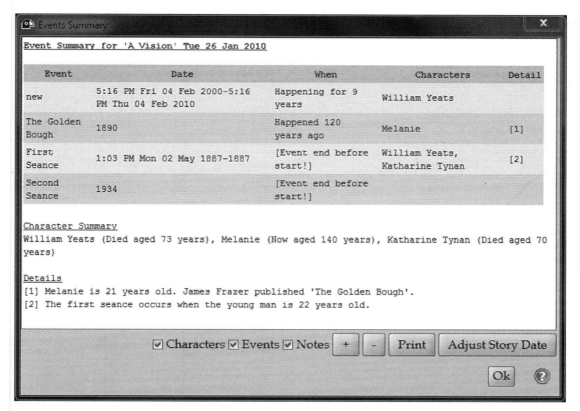

Figure 4.8 Event summary.

Create an Outline

We'll go into more detail about exporting your story in Chapter 7, page 96. But now is a good time to show you how to create and print a story outline.

In a way, you already have an outline of your story in Tree View. But suppose you want to print that outline, as well as customize it to your own formatting specifications.

In general, an outline consists of chapter and scene titles. While WriteItNow also allows you to print other information (text, characters, and so on), let's assume you only want a nice clean layout of your chapters and scenes.

To export the outline to an .rtf, from the Main menu, select Export > Setup Options. Check boxes for Chapter Titles and Numbers and Scene Titles and Numbers (Figure 4.9). Click OK.

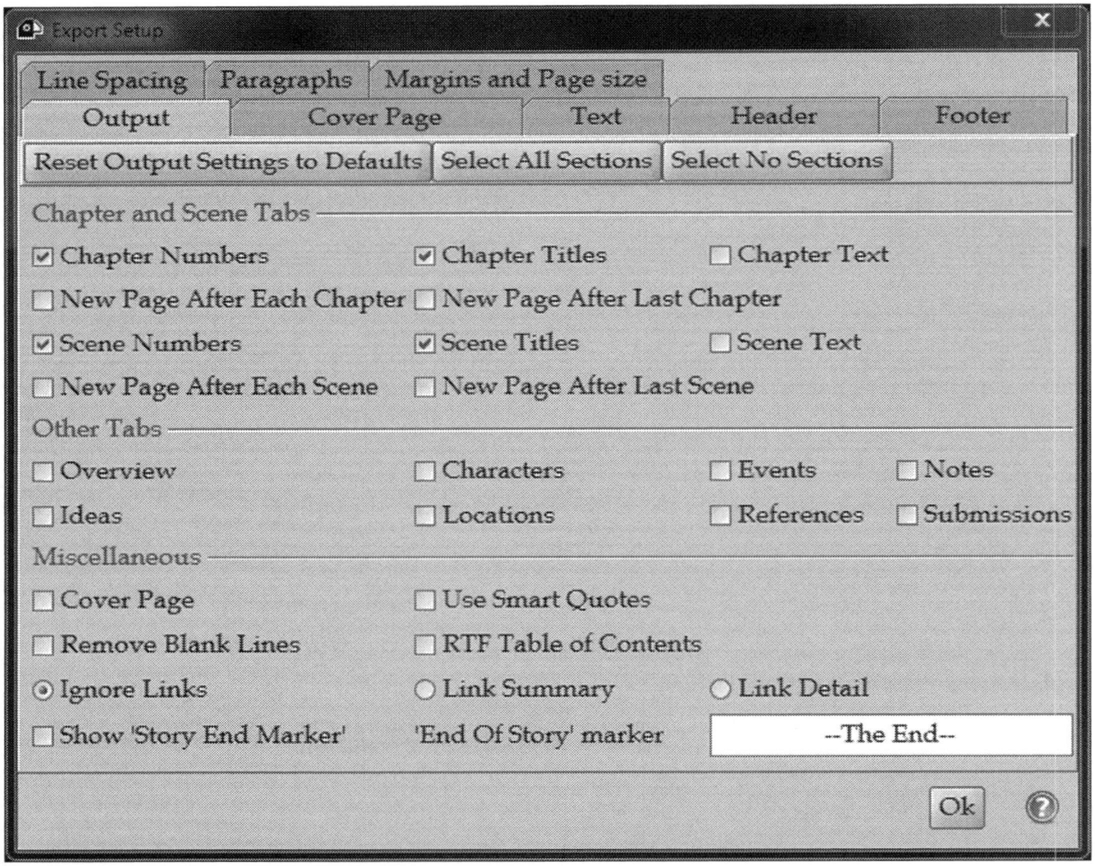

Figure 4.9 Export outline settings.

Then from the Main menu, select Export > Story as RTF. After a moment, for PC users, your new .rtf file will open in your default word processor for viewing or printing (Figure 4.10). For Mac users, open your word processor and load the exported .rtf file.

It could be said equally well that most stories (and novels too) have plots of the errand of search.

—Eudora Welty

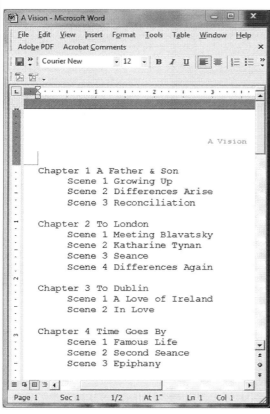

Figure 4.10 Exported story outline.

GO TO AN EVENT

Double click on an Event to go to that Event.

I wonder why, on such a day as this, when the story is particularly clear in my head, I have a kind of virginal reluctance to get to it. I seem to want to think about it and moon about it for a very long time before I get down to it. Today, I think I know one of the main reasons. Today's work is so important I am afraid of it.

—John Steinbeck

WINDOW POSITION

WriteItNow remembers the screen position of dialog boxes. Move them to your preferred location, and they will reappear there each time you use them.

CREATE AN OUTLINE

CHAPTER 5 Enhance Your Story

You climb a long ladder until you can see over the roof, or over the clouds. You are writing a book. You watch your shod feet step on each round rung, one at a time; you do not hurry and do not rest.

—Annie Dillard

WriteItNow contains many essential tools for working with your story. In this section, we'll show you how to use them.

WRITING TOOLS

Familiarize yourself with WriteItNow's useful writing tools:

Word Count

Story Readability

Statistics

Global Find

Global Replace

Thesaurus/Dictionary

Spelling Checker

Insert Accent/Symbol

Word Count

Use Word Count to keep track of your writing progress and to gauge your story length to a target that you or your publisher has set. Access Word Count from the Main menu; select Tools > Story Word Count (or Ctrl-F1). A pop-up window displays three word counts: Scene Text, Chapter Text, and Chapter + Scene Text (Figure 5.1; Table 5.1). To find individual scene word counts, see page 59.

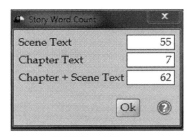

Figure 5.1 Word Count.

Readability

Use Readability metrics to gauge the reading level of your story. Access Readability from the Main menu; select Tools > Story Readability (or Ctrl-F2). A pop-up window displays the readability level for each scene and chapter and for the entire story (Figure 5.2)

Table 5.1 Word Count Terminology

Scene Text	number of words in all scene text (all scenes for all chapters summed)
Chapter Text	number of words in all chapter details text
Chapter + Scene Text	number of words in all scenes plus all chapter details

The Story Readability window displays the average age required to read the text. For example, a readability of 12.3 is appropriate for a person that is roughly 12 years and four months old. See Table 5.2 for conversions among readability, ages, and corresponding US, UK, and Scottish grade levels.

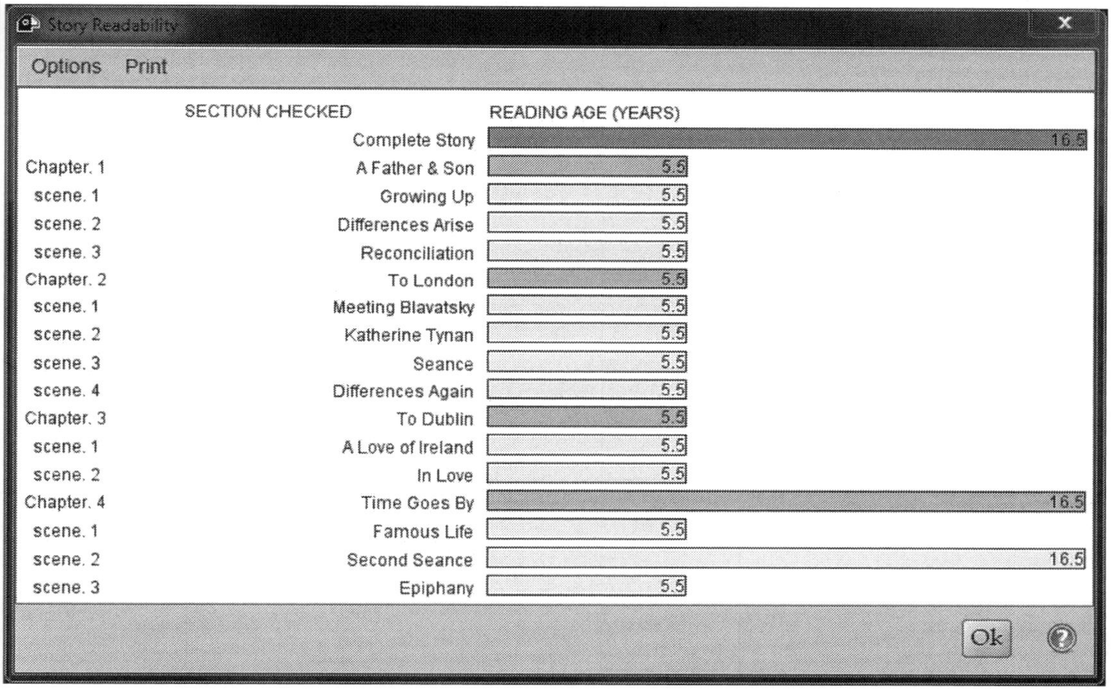

Figure 5.2 Story Readability.

Table 5.2 FRE readability and equivalent ages and grade levels.

		Grade Level Equivalents		
FRE	Age	US	UK	Scottish
90-100	10-11	5th grade	key stage 2	P7
80-90	11-12	6th grade	key stage 3	S1
70-80	12-13	7th grade	key stage 4	S2
60-70	13-15	8th-9th grade	key stage 3-4	S3-4
50-60	15-18	10-12th grade	key stage 4-level A	S5-6
30-50	18-21		college undergraduate	
0-30	21+		college graduate	

Scene Readability

To obtain a more detailed analysis of a focal scene's readability, in the scene's editing toolbar, select Tools > Check Readability (or Ctrl-Q). The pop-up window displays word count, words per sentence, sentence count, average syllables per word, and total syllables (Figure 5.3).

Two readability metrics are given: Flesch-Kincaid Grade Level and the Flesch Reading Ease (Figure 5.3). Both metrics are calculated using syllable, word, and sentence counts. These readability metrics can be translated into ages using Table 5.2. In addition, to put the readability metric into context, WriteItNow compares the reading level to a type of text you

Table 5.3 FRE scores for familiar writing samples.

Sample	Score
Comics	92
Consumer ads in magazines	82
Movie Screen	75
Seventeen	67
Reader's Digest	65
Sports Illustrated	63
New York Daily News	60
Atlantic Monthly	57
Time	52
Newsweek	50
Wall Street Journal	43
Harvard Business Review	43
New York Times	39
New York Review of Books	35
Harvard Law Review	32
Standard auto insurance policy	10
Internal Revenue Code	-6

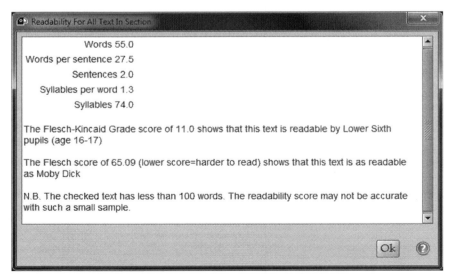

Figure 5.3 Scene Readability.

may be familiar with (Table 5.3).

To view word count together with readability for a particular scene, in the scene editing tool bar, select Tools > Word Count. You can also use Ctrl-W, or click the Word Count button (Figure 5.4). A "Statistics for Scene" pop-up window will display Story Word Count, Chapter and Scenes Word Count, Scene Word Count, Number of Sentences in Scene, and Scene Reading Age (Table 5.4).

Table 5.4 Scene Statistics.

Story Word Count	words in all scenes plus chapter details
Chapter & Scenes Word Count	words in all scenes plus chapter details for the focal chapter only
Scene Word Count	words in the focal scene only
Number of Sentences in Scene	sentences in the focal scene only
Scene Reading Age	reading age for the focal scene only

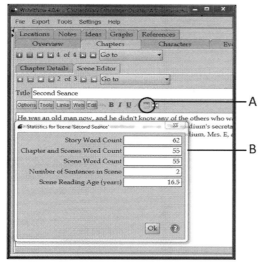

Figure 5.4 Scene Statistics. **A.** Word count button, **B.** Statistics pop-up window.

READABILITY & WORD COUNT OF SELECTED TEXT

You can get the readability of any section of text by highlighting it and then selecting Tools > Check Readability.

To get the word count of any section of text, highlight it and select Tools > Word Count.

SCENE READABILITY

Global Find & Replace

Use Global Find to find all the occurrences of a particular word or phrase in your story. To access Global Find, from the Main menu, select Tools > Global Find (or Ctrl-F10). A dialog box pops up (Figure 5.5). Type in the word you want to find. Note that the word used in the last search appears by default in the Find box drop-down. Check the appropriate boxes if you want the search to be case sensitive or for whole words only.

For example, if you want to find "son," check Whole Words if you want to exclude words like sonogram and grandson. When you click Find, the Global Find results are summarized (Figure 5.5). Double-click any of the results to go directly to that occurrence of your search word in your story. You can leave the find box open while you peruse the results, shifting back and forth between the find results and your story text. Click OK to finish your search and close the find box.

Use Global Replace to replace all occurrences of a particular word or phrase with another word or phrase. For example, you may want to change a character's name throughout your entire story. Suppose you'd like to refer to Katharine Tynan as "Miss Tynan" instead of "Katharine." To be on the safe side, first do a simple Global Find to check all the occurrences of Katharine. If you're satisfied with replacing *all* of these occurrences, then do the Global Replace.

From the Main menu, select Tools > Global Replace (or Ctrl-F11). In the dialog pop-up window, specify the word or phrase you want to find, as well as the word or phrase you want as a replacement (Figure 5.6). For example, Find

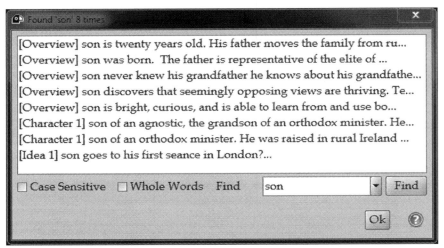

Figure 5.5 Global Find.

"Katharine" and Replace with "Miss Tynan." Specify whether you want the find and replace to be case sensitive and/or to find whole words only.

After you select Replace All, a warning window pops up. The warning will ask you whether you want to replace *every* occurrence of the word/phrase. The warning screen reminds you that "This cannot be undone!" There is NO UNDO for this action! Be sure you've clicked whole words when replacing a word like "son,"

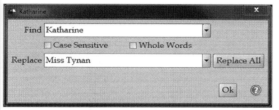

Figure 5.6 Global Replace.

which occurs within many other words besides "son." Click Yes to accept all replacements. You will not be asked to okay each replacement individually.

Thesaurus

The WriteItNow Thesaurus provides a plethora of information about words. It contains over 150,000 words and definitions, which are all cross-indexed. The data for the thesaurus are supplied by WordNet 2.0.

To use the thesaurus, from any Tab View editing toolbar, select Tools > Thesaurus (or Ctrl-T). Alternatively, from the Main menu, select Tools > Thesaurus (or Ctrl-F4).

If a word is highlighted when you invoke the thesaurus, that word will be looked up (Figure 5.7A). The default thesaurus setting shows you

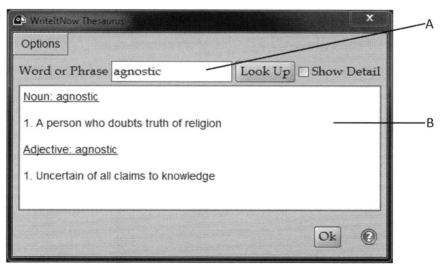

Figure 5.7 Thesaurus. **A.** Word that was selected in text or word you type in, **B.** Click on words in this box to get their definitions.

the word's definition. When you've opened the thesaurus, you may also type a word in the Word or Phrase box to get its definition. To look up a word within the definition, double-click it (Figure 5.7B).

To get more information about the word you selected, check the Show Detail box. (Figure 5.8; Table 5.5) Use the detailed information to enrich your writing by seeking the most appropriate word for each situation. The thesaurus helps you learn about words and their meanings in broader contexts. You can find word plays, double entendres, and improve your vocabulary.

You can also use WriteItNow's thesaurus to solve crossword puzzles and to find rhymes and other similar-sounding words.

For example, suppose you only know some

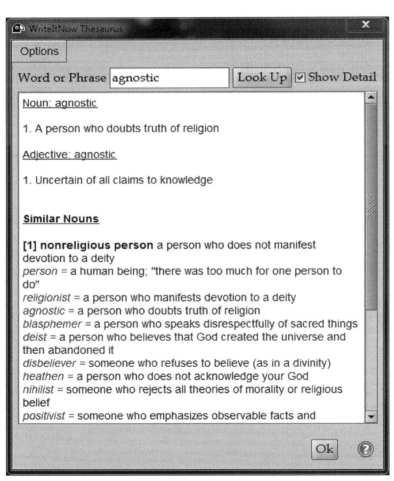

Figure 5.8 Thesaurus detail information.

Table 5.5 Explanation of Thesaurus Show Detail terms.

Antonym	Two words which are opposites are antonyms of each other (e.g., "short" and "long."
Attribute	A noun for which adjectives express values. For example, the noun "weight" is an attribute. The adjectives "light" and "heavy" are two of its possible values.
Entailment	A verb X entails Y if X cannot be performed unless Y is or has been performed.
Meronym	When one thing is part of another. X is a meronym of Y if X is a part of Y. For example, "flour" is a meronym of "cake."
Holonym	The name of the whole of which the meronym names a part. Y is a holonym of X if X is a part of Y. For example "table" is a holonym of "leg."
Hypernym	A term for a group of specific instances. Y is a hypernym of X if X is a (kind of) Y. For example, "dog" is a hypernym of "dalmatian" because a dalmatian is a kind of dog.
Coordinate	Nouns or verbs that have the same hypernym. For example, "dalmatian" and "labrador" are coordinate terms because they have the same hypernym ("dog").

of the letters of a word in a crossword. Type them, using a period (.) as a placeholder for any single missing letters. Use an asterisk (*) when you know that at least one letter is missing. The thesaurus will display possible matches for your specifications (Figure 5.9).

For example, if you type "c.t" and press Enter (or Look Up), the thesaurus will display: [1] cat [2] cot [3] crt [4] cst [5] cut [6] cwt. Double-click on any of these words to get its definition. If you type "p*t," the thesaurus will display: [1] pabst [2] pacific coast [3] pacific halibut [4] pacific newt, and so on.

You can combine letters, asterisks, and periods in any order. For example, "bo*t.e" will find: [1] boar thistle [2] boat whistle [3] bog

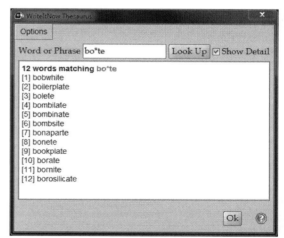

Figure 5.9 Use the WriteItNow thesaurus to solve crosswords.

myrtle [4] bola tie [5] bolo tie [6] bombardier beetle [7] bootee [8] bootie [9] bottle [10] bow tie [11] box turtle.

THESAURUS

Spelling Checker

Use WriteItNow's Spelling Checker to check the spelling of each editor window individually.

From the editing toolbar, select Tools > Spelling Checker (or Ctrl-L). The misspelled word will appear in the Not in Dictionary Box (Figure 5.10) and also in the Word in Context box, showing the phrase in which the word occurs. For each mispelled word (*i.e.*, not in WriteItNow's dictionary), WriteItNow will suggest replacements. Select a replacement by clicking it. The new word will appear in the Replacement box. Click Change to change this occurrence or Change All to change all occurrences. After clicking Add to Dictionary, Ignore (All), or Change (All), WriteItNow will continue to the next misspelling.

Insert Accented Character

To insert accents and other symbols, from the editing toolbar, select Tools > Insert Accented Character (or Ctrl-K). Click on the accented character or symbol to add it to your text (Figure 5.11).

Figure 5.11 Insert accent or symbol.

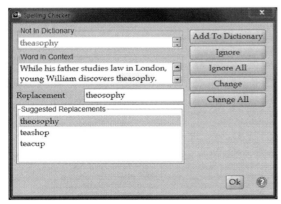

Figure 5.10 Spelling Checker.

Dictionaries

WriteItNow has three dictionaries: Canadian English, UK English, and United States English. To choose your dictionary, from the Main menu, select Settings > Tool Settings > Set Main Dictionary. Four dictionary files (.dict) will appear (Figure 5.12). Choose Canadian (en_CA), UK (en_GB), or United States (en_US). The fourth dictionary "user.dict" contains words that you've added to the dictionary.

You can use other dictionaries as well. The dictionary must be plain text and have one word per line in alphabetical order. These are often called "word lists." For example:

Apple

Apricot

Book

...

Zygote.

To use another dictionary (or word list), do the following:

1. Place the word list/dictionary in your install folder in the "dictionary" directory (for example, c:\writeitnow4\dictionary).

2. Rename it so it ends with ".dict" (for example, french.dict).

3. Run WriteItNow.

4. Select Settings > Tool Settings > Set Main dictionary.

5. Select the new dictionary.

The new dictionary will now be used as the main dictionary.

Regardless of the main dictionary you use, when you add a word, it will be added to the

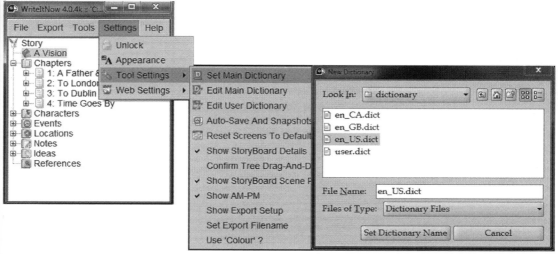

Figure 5.12 Select Dictionary.

user dictionary (user.dict). You can add words to your user dictionary during a spell check and from the Main menu.

To add (or delete) words from your user dictionary, from the Main menu, select Settings > Tool Settings > Edit User Dictionary. For example, in the figure below, we've added the word "rood" (a word used by William Yeats in a phrase, "by the rood") to our user dictionary (Figure 5.13).

Although it's safer to restrict your edits to the user dictionary, you can edit one of the three main dictionaries (CA, UK, or US) as follows: From the Main menu, select Settings > Tool Settings > Edit Main Dictionary (Figure 5.13).

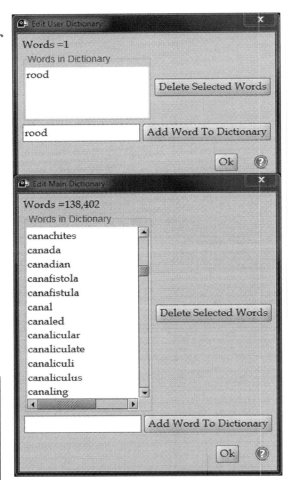

Figure 5.13 Edit User (*Above*) or Main (*Below*) dictionaries.

What this means, in practical terms for the student writer, is that in order to achieve mastery he must read widely and deeply and must write not just carefully but continually, thoughtfully assessing and reassessing what he writes, because practice, for the writer as for the concert pianist, is the heart of the matter.

—John Gardner

Web Tools

As you've seen, WriteItNow has a powerful built-in dictionary and thesaurus. But you can also use WriteItNow to directly link to the internet to explore additional information. You can link to web searches, image searches, online dictionaries, online thesauruses, online encyclopedias, online quote databases, and online rhyming dictionaries.

Access these web tools from the editing toolbar by clicking the Web button and selecting one of the web options (Figure 5.14). Or use one of the hot keys.

After selecting a web option, type the word or phrase you want to find in the Text to Look Up box. Optionally, you can select from the list of words you've previously searched for. Click OK.

For example, say you want to learn more about Katharine Tynan. We think she might have been a young lover or confident of W. B. Yeats. To see what an online encyclopedia says about her, from the editing toolbar, select Web > Encyclopedia. Type in Katharine Tynan, and click OK (Figure 5.15). WriteItNow opens your web browser and takes you to the Wikipedia search result (Figure 5.15). The other web tools work similarly.

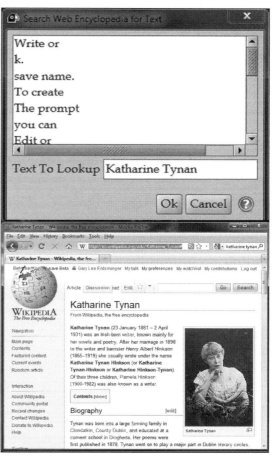

Figure 5.15 Web encyclopedia search box (*Above*) and search result (*Below*).

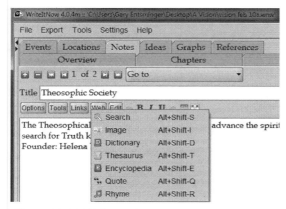

Figure 5.14 Web options.

You can also customize or update web settings. For example, if you have a subscription to an online dictionary, you can direct WriteItNow to take you there instead of to the default online dictionary. If a site updates its URL, you can update the WriteItNow link to avoid an error message.

To change where a web tool takes you, from the Main menu, select Settings > Web Settings. Click the web tool you want to change.

For example, suppose you want to have WriteItNow take you to the Merriam-Webster Unabridged, where you have an online subscription (instead of the default Wiktionary dictionary). Take the following steps:

1. From the Main menu, select Settings > Web Settings > Dictionary (5.16A). A window will pop up (5.16B).

2. Open a web browser and navigate to the Merriam-Webster page. Log in.

3. Copy and paste the Merriam-Webster URL into the WriteItNow box titled "Web Page URL To Visit" (5.16C).

4. Look up a word in your browser, for example "visionary"(5.16D), and re-examine the URL (5.16E).

5. Find the text added after the home URL and before the word you searched for. Add this code to the WriteItNow box titled "Command Before Text" (5.15F).

6. Find the text added after the word you searched for. Add this code to the WriteItNow box titled "Command After Text" (5.15G).

7. Click OK. The next time you use the Web Dictionary, your word will automatically be looked up in the new dictionary (*e.g.*, Merriam-Webster).

You can also change Web Settings if a site has been updated since you purchased your copy of WriteItNow. For example, the online thesaurus is found at this URL: http://wordnetweb. princeton.edu/perl/webwn. By default, some older WriteItNow versions linked to a now out of date URL for the Web Thesaurus (http:// wordnet.princeton.edu/perl/webwn). Thus, if you have an older version of WriteItNow, you might need to reset the default Web Thesaurus. To do so, follow these steps:

1. From the Main menu, select Settings > Web Settings Thesaurus.

2. In the Web Page URL To Visit box, type in the new URL: http://wordnetweb. princeton.edu/perl/webwn.

3. Click OK.

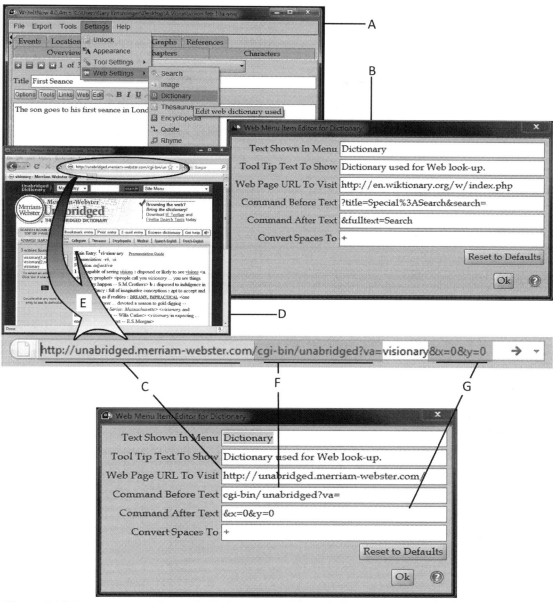

Figure 5.16 How to customize web dictionary. **A.** Edit web dictionary, **B.** Default web dictionary settings, **C.** New home page URL, **D.** Search for a word, **E.** Examine new URL, **F.** Copy command before search word (after home URL), **G.** Copy command after search word.

WEB TOOLS

Web Links

WriteItNow Links create shortcuts from text in an editor window, such as a scene or note, to where you've stored more information. You can link to webpages, files on your computer, or to other areas (*i.e.,* other components) within your WriteItNow file.

Add links from an editor window. From the Links button drop down menu, select the type of link you want to create (Figure 5.17A).

To create a link to a webpage, you should first have the webpage open. For example, open the wikipedia page where we searched for Katharine Tynan (page 67). Highlight the webpage URL and copy: Right-click > Copy, or Edit > Copy. (Figure 5.17B). In the desired editor window in WriteItNow, select Links > Web Links (or Alt-W). Paste the copied URL into the dialog box (Figure 5.17C) and click OK.

A link will now appear in the scene editor (Figure 5.17D). When you hover your cursor over the link symbol, it will indicate the URL of the link. You can also enter text to tell you something more informative about the link.

When you click the link symbol, you're given the option to Launch the link (a browser will open with the linked page). You may also delete or edit the link.

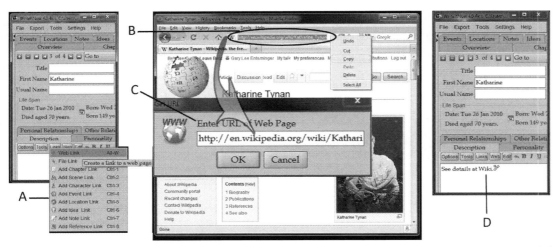

Figure 5.17 Web links. **A.** Drop-down web link menu, **B.** Copy URL into web link dialog box (*C*), **D.** Web link appears in editor window.

DEFAULT WEB SETTINGS

Search	Google Web
Image	Google Images
Dictionary	Wiktionary
Thesaurus	WordNetWeb
Encyclopedia	Wikipedia
Quote	The Quotations Page
Rhyme	RhymeZone

To me as a story writer, generalizations about writing come tardily and uneasily, and I would limit them, if I were wise, by saying that any conclusions I feel confidence in are stuck to the particular story, part of the animal. The most trustworthy lesson I've learned from work so far is the simple one that the writing of each story is sure to open up a different prospect and pose a new problem.

—Eudora Welty

WEB HOT KEYS

Search	Alt+Shift+S
Image	Alt+Shift+I
Dictionary	Alt+Shift+D
Thesaurus	Alt+Shift+T
Encyclopedia	Alt+Shift+E
Quote	Alt+Shift+Q
Rhyme	Alt+Shift+R

Well, I think that a serious fiction writer describes an action only in order to reveal a mystery.

—Flannery O'Connor

WEB LINKS

File Links

For PCs only, use File Links to run other computer programs outside WriteItNow. For example, if you link to a Word document, when you click the link it will open Microsoft Word and load the document. You could also link to an .mp3 file if there is music or a speech referenced in your story. Then when you click on the link, your .mp3 player starts and plays the .mp3. Listen to get in the mood for this section of your story. Create a soundtrack.

To link to a file on your computer, from the editing toolbar, select Links > File Link (or Alt-F). Use the pop-up window to navigate to the desired file (Figure 5.18). For example, we want to link to a file we made with notes about several locations in our story. Earlier, we used an outline file we made with NoteTab (Fookes Software).

Select the desired file and click Create Link To Selected File. The file link symbol appears in your editor window (Figure 5.18). If desired, type in some text to remind you what the link is about. As for web links, you can hover your cursor over the symbol to remind you where the link goes. And you can Launch, Delete, or Edit the link by clicking it.

> *I have never known a writer who was not at one time an avid reader. I believe it was T.S. Eliot who said that if a writer has a pretentious literary style, it is generally because he has not read enough books.*
>
> —William S. Burroughs

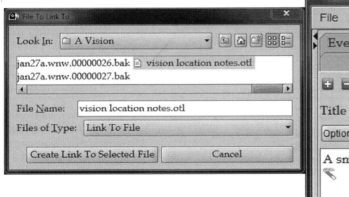

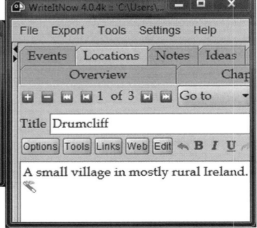

Figure 5.18 File links. File link pop-up window (*Left*), File link added to editor window (*Right*).

Component Links

Imagine you're describing a character while working in the Characters tab editor. Then you realize that some text you put in a note is relevant to your character. Add a link to the note.

To link to another component within WriteItNow, from the editing toolbar, select Links, and click the type of link you want to create. For example, to link to information about a particular location, click Add Location Link (or Ctrl-5) (Figure 5.19A).

Choose a location you want to link to and click OK (Figure 5.19B). The location link symbol now appears in your editor window (Figure 5.19C). Type in reminder text or put your cursor over the symbol to see what the symbol links to.

You have four choices if you click the link. "Go to" will move you to that linked location.

"Delete Link" will remove the link. "Expand Summary" will replace the link with the title of the linked location. "Expand Link Detail" will replace the link with all the text from your linked location.

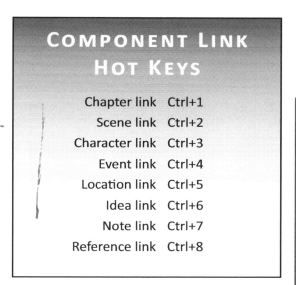

COMPONENT LINK HOT KEYS

Chapter link	Ctrl+1
Scene link	Ctrl+2
Character link	Ctrl+3
Event link	Ctrl+4
Location link	Ctrl+5
Idea link	Ctrl+6
Note link	Ctrl+7
Reference link	Ctrl+8

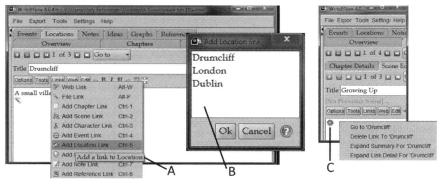

Figure 5.19 Location link. **A.** Component link menu, **B.** Choose location, **C.** Location link added to editor window.

COMPONENT LINKS

REFERENCES

We all need to know when, what, and who we learned from. Let others know, so they too can learn from your resources.

Writing is, for most, laborious and slow. The mind travels faster than the pen; consequently, writing becomes a question of learning to make occasional wing shots, bringing down the bird of thought as it flashes by.

—William Strunk Jr. and E.B. White

References

Use the References tab to keep a record of the references you've used while researching your story (Figure 5.20). To add a reference, in the References tab, click the ➕ button (Figure 5.20A). Fill in the Title and click Add Author (Figure 5.20B,C). Type in the author's name in the pop-up window (Figure 5.20D). Click OK.

You can also add other reference details (*e.g.,* a page reference, publication date, and other text; Figure 5.20F,H,I). Click on the calendar button to add the publication date (Figure 5.20G). WriteItNow shows how this reference will be displayed after you export (Figure 5.20J).

You can export references with your story (from Main menu Export, see Chapter 7; page 96). Alternatively, you can export references directly from the References tab. Click the Options button (Figure 5.20E) and select the desired type of export (.rtf, .pdf, .html, .txt). When PC users click the export type, their references will automatically open in the selected format's program. Mac users need to run the program and load the exported file.

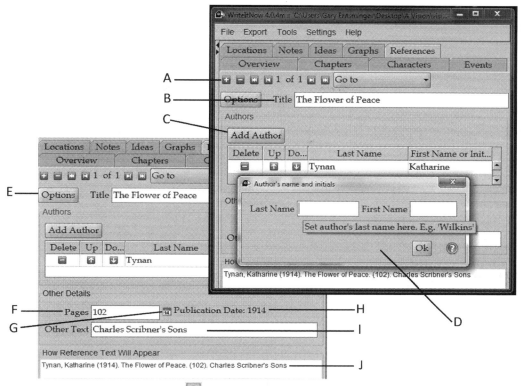

Figure 5.20 References. **A.** Click to add a reference, **B.** Reference title, **C.** Add author, **D.** Author po-up window, **E.** Export options, **F.** Pages, **G.** Calendar button, **H.** Publication date, **I.** Other text, **J.** How reference will appear.

CHAPTER 6 Features to Inspire Creativity

My earliest memory is of imagining I was someone else—imagining that I was, in fact, the Ringling Brothers Circus Strongboy.

—Stephen King

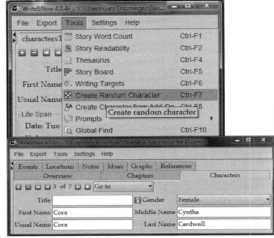

Figure 6.1 Create random character navigation (*Above*) and dialog box (*Below*).

Character Generators

Use WriteItNow Character Generators to create new characters or to develop existing characters. WriteItNow has two types of character generators: Random and Add-On.

When you create a Random Character (Main menu: Tools > Create Random Character, or Ctrl-F7), the resulting character is given a random name (Figure 6.1). You then define the rest of the character's characteristics, relationships, and so on.

Use Create Character from Add-On when you want WriteItNow to help you generate more information about the character (name, personality, description, and historical context).

From the Main menu, select Tools > Create Character from Add-On (or Ctrl-F8). A window pops up with areas for you to fill in with WriteItNow's help (Figure 6.2). To create an add-on character, you must at least generate a name. You can also add personality, description, and timeline data.

Character Add-On: Name

First, create your character's name. Click the ① Name button to open the Name Picker window (Figure 6.3). Under Name Data, select a nationality, or select All to randomly pick names from different nationalities. Note that you can't create a biblical last name since people in the Bible didn't have them. Select Male or Female. If you know which letter you want a name to start with, type it in the Name Start Box.

For example, let's say we want a British female whose first name starts with the letter M. Click Create First to generate a name. If you don't like that name, keep clicking until you find a name you like. The generated names

CHARACTER GENERATORS

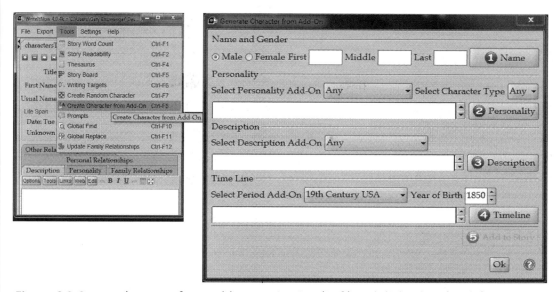

Figure 6.2 Create character from add-on navigation (*Left*) and dialog box (*Right*).

are saved in the Generated Names box. Select a name from the list if you prefer a name you previously generated. Continue creating middle and last names in the same manner. Or create all three names at once by clicking Create All.

When you're satisfied with the name (*i.e.*, the name that appears in the Current Name boxes), click Use Current Name to save the name and return to the Character Add-On Details window (Figure 6.3).

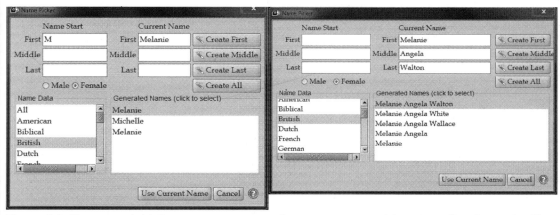

Figure 6.3 Character Add-On name generator. Generate name with a given first letter (*Left*). Generate entire (first, middle, last) name (*Right*).

CHARACTER ADD-ON: NAME

Character Add-On: Personality

Define your character's personality. If you want WriteItNow to pick a random personality for you, click **②** Personality (Figure 6.2), and a random personality will appear in the Personality box. If you want more control over your character's personality, select the Select Personality Add-On drop down list, which is set at Any for the default. Choose from three well-known personality classifications: Archetype, Anneagram, or Myers-Briggs (Table 6.1). After selecting a classifying system, select a Character Type that falls within one of these systems (or leave it at Any to let WriteItNow randomly choose a character type).

Once you've selected a personality classification and type, click **②** Personality to see the personality description generated by WriteItNow. Keep clicking **②** Personality to generate different personality descriptions (all will adhere to the classification and type you selected).

Character Add-On: Description

Let WriteItNow help you describe your character's general appearance. Choose your characters relative age (Normal or Old) or let WriteItNow select an age (Any) (Figure 6.2). Click **③** Description to generate an age-specific description. Continue clicking **③** Description until you find one you like.

NAME GENERATOR

If you already know a lot about your character, but you need help picking a name, use Create Character from Add-On Name Picker to generate first, middle, and last names of specified nationalities.

Remarkably material also is the writer's attempt to control his own energies so he can work. He must be sufficiently excited to rouse himself to the task at hand, and not so excited he cannot sit down to it.

—Annie Dillard

Table 6.1 Explanation of Character Add-On personality types.

Archetypes	In 1940 Joseph Campbell wrote The "Hero's Journey" in which he identifies seven archetypical character types.
Hero	One who must go on a journey and suffer to complete a task.
Mentor	A wise person who helps or trains the hero.
Threshold Guardian	An important crossing, or a minor antagonist who often provides the first problem for the hero.
Herald	Person (or event) that announces the coming of significant change.
Shapeshifter	Person whose loyalties are unclear or variable.
Shadow	A negative figure (often the antagonist) who represents things we dislike and would like to eliminate.
Trickster	A mischief-maker, clown, or fool that provides light relief and surprises.
Enneagram	The Enneagram divides personalities into nine distinct types, each with a distinguishing set of features.
1: Reformers	Always try to be right.
2: Helpers	Are motivated by helping others.
3: Motivators	See life as challenging and need to win.
4: Romantics	Combine sensitivity, emotional intensity, and intuition.
5: Thinkers	Try to explain the world.
6: Loyalists	Need to trust others and be trusted.
7: Enthusiasts	Are adventurous, exuberant, and have wide interests.
8: Confronters	Are assertive, speak their minds, and make quick decisions.
9: Mediators	Are patient and good listeners.
Myers-Briggs	Carl Jung developed a theory of psychological types based on the four pairs of attributes (1: E/I Extroverted or Introverted, 2: N/S Intuitive or Sensing, 3: F/T Feeling or Thinking, and 4: P/J Perceiving or Judging). For example, ENFP = Extroverted-Intuitive-Feeling-Perceiving.

ENFP	Enthusiast	ESFP	Performer
INFP	Idealist	ISFP	Artist
ENFJ	Teacher	ESFJ	Protector
INFJ	Counselor	ISFJ	Nurturer
ENTP	Innovator	ESTP	Promoter
INTP	Thinker	ISTP	Mechanic
ENTJ	Executive	ESTJ	Supervisor
INTJ	Scientist	ISTJ	Inspector

CHARACTER ADD-ON: DESCRIPTION

Character Add-On: Timeline

To create some historical context for your character, first select a Period Add-On (Figure 6.2). You can choose among one of four time periods (Table 6.2).

Select the year your character was born, then click **Timeline**. A timeline of events appears. (Figure 6.4). The year of each even is given. Next to each year, WriteItNow displays the number of years before or after your character's birth that this event took place. There is also a check-box next to each timeline event. Click the events that you want to remember to give your new character context. Then click OK. The events will now appear in the Timeline box. You can, optionally, add these timeline events to the Events tab in your story (page 82).

Table 6.2 Explanation of Character Add-On background timeline information.

20th Century America	Political, social, scientific, and artistic events that shaped the USA in the 20th Century and the beginning of the 21st Century.
19th Century America	Political, social, scientific, and artistic events that shaped the USA in the 19th Century.
Victorian Britain	Events that shaped Britain in the age of Queen Victoria and Charles Dickens.
Tudor Britain	Important events in the age of Queen Elizabeth I and Shakespeare.
Stuart Britain	Important events in the age of Charles II and Cromwell. Notes on the Civil War and the Great Fire.

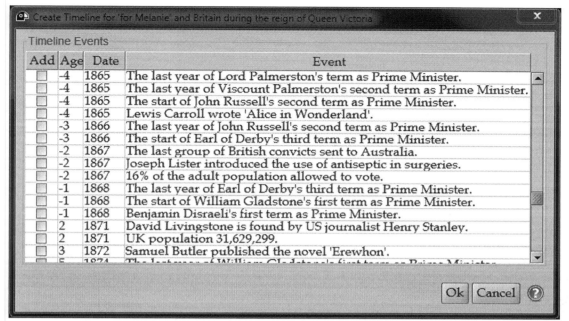

Figure 6.4 Character Add-On background timeline data.

> *Life is... a luminous halo, a semi-transparent envelope surrounding us from the beginning of consciousness to the end. Is it not the task of the novelist to convey this varying, this unknown and uncircumscribed spirit?*
>
> —Virginia Woolf

Character Add-On: Complete

When you're satisfied with your new character, click 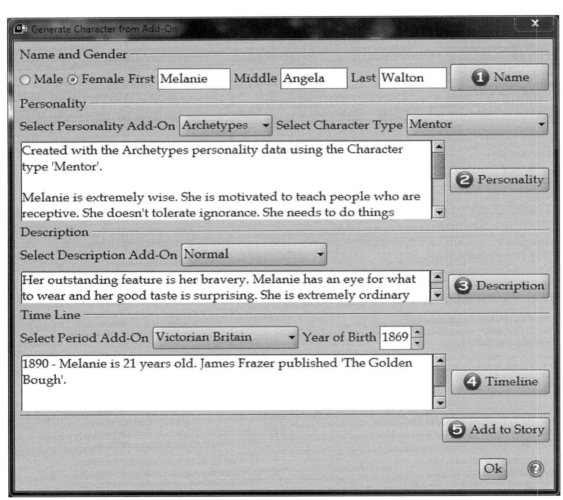 Add to Story (Figure 6.5). If you've selected timeline events, a window pops up to ask you if you want the events added to your Events tab. After you select Yes or No, a window pops up to confirm that your new character has been added.

From the Main menu, select File > Downloads to get the newest add-ons and prompt sets from Ravenshead Services.

Figure 6.5 Completed Character created from Add-On.

Idea Generator

Suppose you've temporarily run out of ideas. (Yep, it happens.) WriteItNow's Idea Generator can help. It's fun to use, as it helps you generate scandalous events, personality quirks, clever situations, thoughtful character responses, and much more. The Idea Generator is customized to your characters and the themes in your story. The farther along you are in your story (*i.e.,* the more characters, the more events, and so on that you've described), the more helpful the Idea Generator becomes. For example, when generating character interactions, it helps if you've defined your characters' genders.

From the Idea T tab editing toolbar, click the Options > Create Idea button (Figure 6.6). Note that you don't need to add an idea (by clicking the button); the generator will automatically add the new idea to your story.

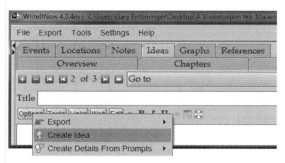

Figure 6.6 Navigation to Idea Generator.

In the pop-up dialog window (Figure 6.7), select the character(s) you want your idea to revolve around. The Idea Generator focuses on one or two characters at a time. So check one or two characters. However, if you're really interested in a diversity of ideas being generated, select more characters and see what happens.

For example, suppose that we haven't figured out how to incorporate Helena Blavatsky, the renowned psychic and founder of the Theosophical Society, into our story ("A Vision"). So let's generate an idea about Helena Blavatsky and our main character, William Yeats. We can choose among different types of ideas: Random, Leisure, Misc., Relationship, Crime, Location, Money, Work, Event, Meeting, or Personal. Let's try a Relationship idea (Figure 6.7).

Once you've chosen characters and idea type, click Generate New Idea. Text will appear in the Current Idea box, usually describing a situation, a question about the situation, and a provoking thought. If you're not sure about this idea, click Generate New Idea again. Your previously generated ideas will be stored in the lower box. You can always return to them by selecting them.

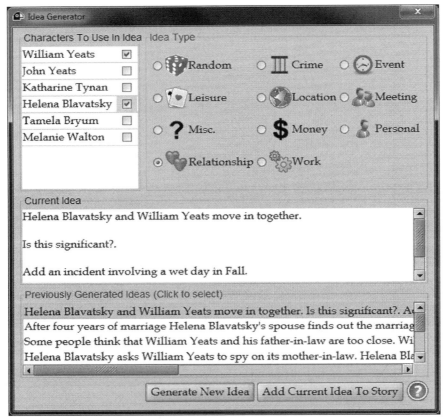

Figure 6.7 Idea Generator dialog.

When you hit on an idea that you like, click Add Current Idea To Story. This generates a new idea with an appropriate title (Figure 6.8). The provoking situation, questions, or thoughts will be added to the idea editor window. Use the space in the editor window to develop this new idea.

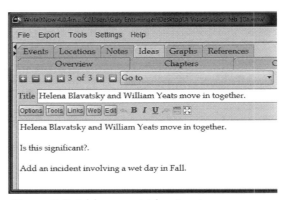

Figure 6.8 Add current idea to story.

Note from Add-On

While idea generators can create interesting situations for characters, WriteItNow's note generator "Note from Add-On" provides factual context (similar to timeline events, page 80) for your story.

Add-Ons are excellent for helping you develop the color of your story and for providing interesting details to improve your story's credibility. Most readers of fiction still like to learn things, and you probably know that non-fiction books are very popular. People enjoy facts. So you can make your story, even if it is fiction, more appealing and engaging by incorporating interesting tidbits of information such as those found in the Note Add-Ons.

To generate a note from an add-on, go to the Notes tab. From the editing toolbar, select Options > Note from Add-On (Figure 6.9). In the pop-up window, you currently have two choices for backgrounds (historical context/time period; Figure 6.10). Select either The Gods of Ancient Egypt or Background information for Britain during the Tudor period (1485 to 1603).

Your story does not need to take place in one of these times or places. History and culture consist of networks of information that defy space and time. For example, the Egyptian god of chaos, Seth, was said to have retired to San Francisco in 1906, the year of the

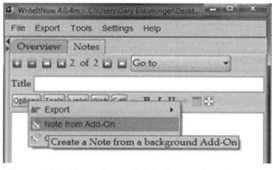

Figure 6.9 Note from Add-On navigation.

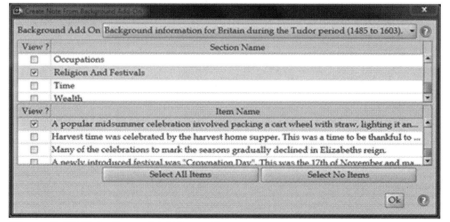

Figure 6.10 Note from Add-On options.

disastrous earthquake. In the popular television show, "Lost," a statue of Sobek, the feared Egyptian god of crocodiles, appears frequently. Lore, celebrations, prejudices, and forms of entertainment in current western society often find their roots in early European traditions, such as those discussed in the Tudor Period Add-On option. For our example, "A Vision," we'll choose Background Tudor information.

Once you've selected a background period, choose the type of information that interests you. From the Tudor period, you can chose one or more of the following categories: Class, Clothes, Entertainment, Food & Drink, Health & Medicine, Measures, Money, Occupations, Religion, Time, and Wealth. From the Ancient Egyptian Gods period, you can choose among The Ennead, Heliopolis, Ra, Isis, and more. We'll choose Religion And Festivals (Figure 6.10).

Possible notes for your selected sections will appear in the lower section of the window (Figure 6.10). Scroll through the notes and select those that you would like to add to your story. Click OK to add the notes to your story. A new idea is automatically generated, titled "Note created from Add-On" (Figure 6.11). You should revise the title to something more specific.

Figure 6.11 Note created from Add-On.

Writing Targets

Another way to motivate your writing is to quantify Flannery O'Connor's advice:

Sit at your desk for three hours each morning. Don't allow yourself to read, answer phone calls, tidy up, or anything else. You sit there. If you are not writing, you still sit there. Eventually, you will write.

Or in other words, set a timer. Set a goal. See how many words you can crank out. Set a personal record. Just type.

WriteItNow facilitates writing goals with its Writing Target feature. Writng Targets are accessed from the Main menu: Tools > Writing Target (or Ctrl-F6) (Figure 6.12).

In the pop-up window (Figure 6.12), first click Reset if you have an old goal still registered. Indicate a time goal (how long you want to "force" yourself to write) and/or a words goal (how many words you'd like to crank out in a set period of time). Click OK and start writing!

Don't worry about the target, it's just a reminder. Focus on writing—use generators and prompts if you're stuck. After typing a while, check your progress. Open the Writing Targets again (Tools > Writing Target, or Ctrl-F6) to see how far you've gotten (Figure 6.12). If you don't reach your goal this time, modify your goal in the future to something more attainable. Gradually increase your goals to challenge yourself.

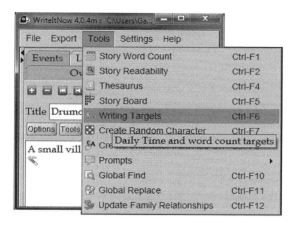

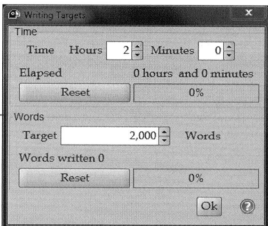

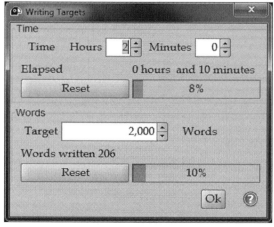

Figure 6.12 Writing targets navigation (*Top*), Goal (*Middle*), and Check (*Bottom*).

Prompt Sets

Prompt Sets are WriteItNow's "question sets" that help develop your story. Think of them as question and answer sessions. See yourself sitting down with a writing instructor or friend who is querying you about your story to help you develop it further. After you go through the prompt interview, you can add the notes you've taken into your story.

WriteItNow Prompt Sets have been created by Ravenshead Services as well as your fellow writers and WriteItNow users. You can create your own prompts and edit existing prompts.

To use a prepared WriteItNow prompt set, from the Main menu, select Tools > Prompts > Use Prompt Set (or Ctrl-F9) (Figure 6.13).

From the Prompt Set Picker pop-up, choose the type of prompt you'd like to work with (Figure 6.13). There are different prompts available to help you develop chapters, scenes, characters, events, ideas, locations, notes, and stories.

Before or after selecting your prompt, open a new component (chapter, scene, character, event, location, note, idea) where you will deposit the information from the prompt after you've completed it.

Prompt sets consist of any combination of "First Steps," "Next Steps," and "Prompts." Each of these (prompts and steps) can do similar things. The prompt author titled them as prompts or steps in an effort to make a cohesive flow to take you through the series of questions. In each prompt or step, there may be a series of questions or statements, and there may or may not be a place for you to type a reply (Figure 6.14). You can type directly into the reply boxes. There may also be "Tips" that appear in yellow conversation bubbles. Click on a Tip, and a window with the tip will pop up.

Once you've gone through the prompt set, you will probably want to save some or all of the

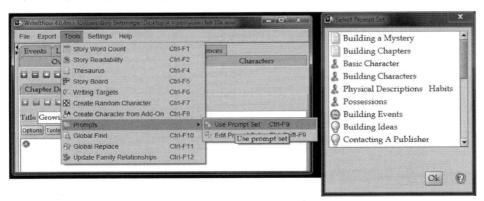

Figure 6.13 Prompt set navigation (*Left*) and selection (*Right*).

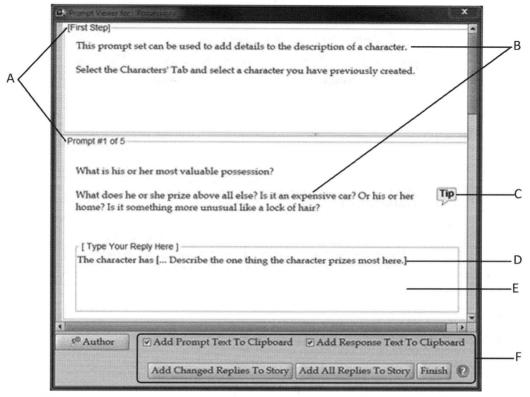

Figure 6.14. Possessions prompt set, showing Two prompts (*A*), Prompt text (*B*), Tip bubble (*C*), Reply help (*D*), Space to reply (*E*), and Add to story options (*F*).

information to your story. WriteItNow provides different options for copying the text in a prompt set (Figure 6.14F). To copy all prompt and response text, simply click Finish (regardless of which boxes you check, all prompts and responses will copy). To copy all prompt text only (no responses), check Add Prompt Text to Clipboard and click Add All Replies To Story. To copy all of your response text only (no prompt text), check Add Response Text to Clipboard and click either button (Add Changed or Add All). To copy prompt and reply text only for prompts where you've made a reply, check both boxes (Add Prompt and Add Response) and click Add Changed. After making your checkbox selection and clicking one of the buttons, all the requested information will be pasted to your clipboard. Paste the information into your story by clicking Ctrl-V.

WriteItNow allows you to customize existing prompts by varying the questions, space for responses, order, and so on. Or you can create new prompts.

Creating questions to ask yourself or other writers in this way (*i.e.,* editing and creating new prompt sets) reminds you to question yourself naturally while writing your story. By creating and answering critical questions, you become a critical thinker. Although it is challenging, critical thinkers can often evaluate their writing with some degree of objectivity. When you learn to this, you can put yourself in a publisher's or editor's shoes. You'll start to make improvements or catch mistakes before others point them out to you.

To edit an existing prompt, from the Main menu, select Tools > Prompts > Edit Prompt Sets (or Ctrl-Shft-F9) (Figure 6.15).

By default, the last prompt you worked on will load. From the Prompt edit main menu, you can Load or Delete an existing prompt (Load, Delete), create a new prompt for any WriteItNow component (New), or save the prompt you're currently editing. You can replace the prompt (Save) or save it as a new prompt (Save As) (Figure 6.16).

Let's revise an existing prompt set. Load the prompt set that you want to edit (or revise) if it's not already loaded. For example, let's revise the Scary Scene prompt set (Figure 6.16).

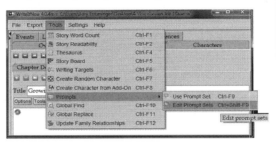

Figure 6.15 Prompt edit navigation.

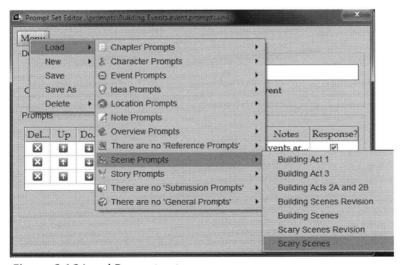

Figure 6.16 Load Prompt set.

In the Details area, rename the prompt set and record your name as the prompt set author to remind yourself that you've contributed to this revision (Figure 6.17). The prompt set type (*i.e.*, scene prompt) is also labeled here.

Before you change the prompt, save it with a new name if you don't want to lose the original prompt. In the Prompt Set Editor window, select Menu > Save As, and revise the prompt set title. Click OK (Figure 6.18).

Use the delete and arrow buttons to delete prompts or change prompt order in the prompt summary (Figure 6.19). Clicking on any of the text cells will open a new window to edit prompt text. The Text box contains the prompt text; it tells the prompt user what to do or think about. If you want the user to respond to the prompt, click the response box. You can get the user started with a response by typing something in the Response Start box. If you type text in the Note box, the text will appear when the user clicks on the Tip bubble. Add additional prompts by clicking the Add New Prompt button. Then fill out the prompt text, and if desired, the Response start and notes.

After you get the feel for using and editing existing prompts, try creating new prompt sets. From Edit Prompt Sets, select Menu > New. Choose the type of prompt set you want to create, name it, and start adding prompts (by clicking in a text cell).

Figure 6.17 Revise prompt details.

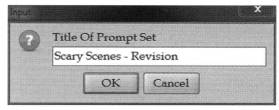

Figure 6.18 Save revised prompt as a new name.

PROMPT SETS

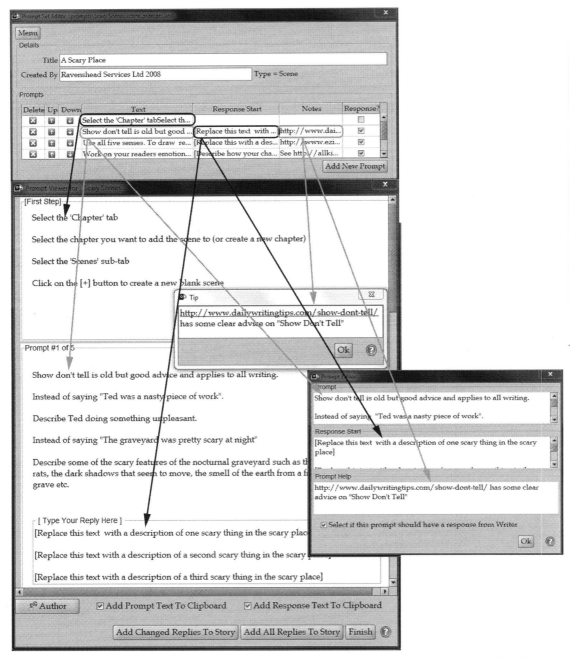

Figure 6.19 Scary Story prompt in user mode (*Bottom Left*), Summary edit mode (*Top*), and Edit mode (*Bottom right*).

FEATURES TO INSPIRE CREATIVITY

Character Generator	Generate a totally random character.
Character Add-On	Create a new character whose characteristics you have some control over.
Character Add-On: Name	Generate a name (first, middle, and last). Specifications include: starting letters, gender, and nationality.
Character Add-On: Personality	Develop a personality based on well-known personality classification systems.
Character Add-On: Description	Generate a character description based on a database of age-specific descriptions.
Character Add-On: Timeline	Provide historical context for your character with WriteItNow's database of political, social, scientific, and artistic events.
Idea Generator	Generate an intriguing situation for characters in your story. Choose from situation types: random, leisure, misc., relationship, crime, location, money, work, event, meeting, or personal.
Note from Add-On	Give your story interesting factual tidbits of information that your readers will love.
Writing Targets	Motivate your creativity by setting goals and monitoring your progress.
Prompt Sets	Critically evaluate your story. Have a mock question-answer interview session relating to your choice of different story components.

EXPORTING & TIPS

CHAPTER 7 Export, E-Book, Print, Submit

> *Go out of your way, if you have to, to look steady and long at the place where earth and sky meet. Likewise, discover the places where your ears can soar out to the edge of audibility. Find a lull in the evening, a valley, a distant remove, a quiet dawn, and listen into that boundary. You can disappear beyond it into where you really live.*

—W.A. Mathieu

To print your story, first export it. When you export, you create a file from all or parts of your story. This file can then by loaded into another program and printed there.

Export Setup

Before exporting your story to another file type, assign your export settings (Main menu > Export > Export Setup Options) (Figure 7.1). These setup options will apply to whatever file type you decide to export (page 103).

WriteItNow has divided Export Setup Options into eight tabs (Figure 7.2). Let's step through each one, noting the choices you should know about.

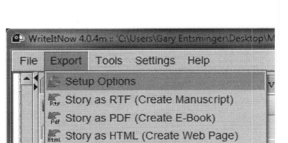

Figure 7.1 Navigation to Export setup.

EXPORT INDIVIDUAL COMPONENTS

Export an individual component, such as a chapter or scene, by selecting the Options button within the component and choosing Export.

"SMART QUOTES"

Unlike plain straight quotes, smart quotes are curved. If you select Smart Quotes when exporting to an .rtf file, WriteItNow will convert your plain quotes to smart quotes.

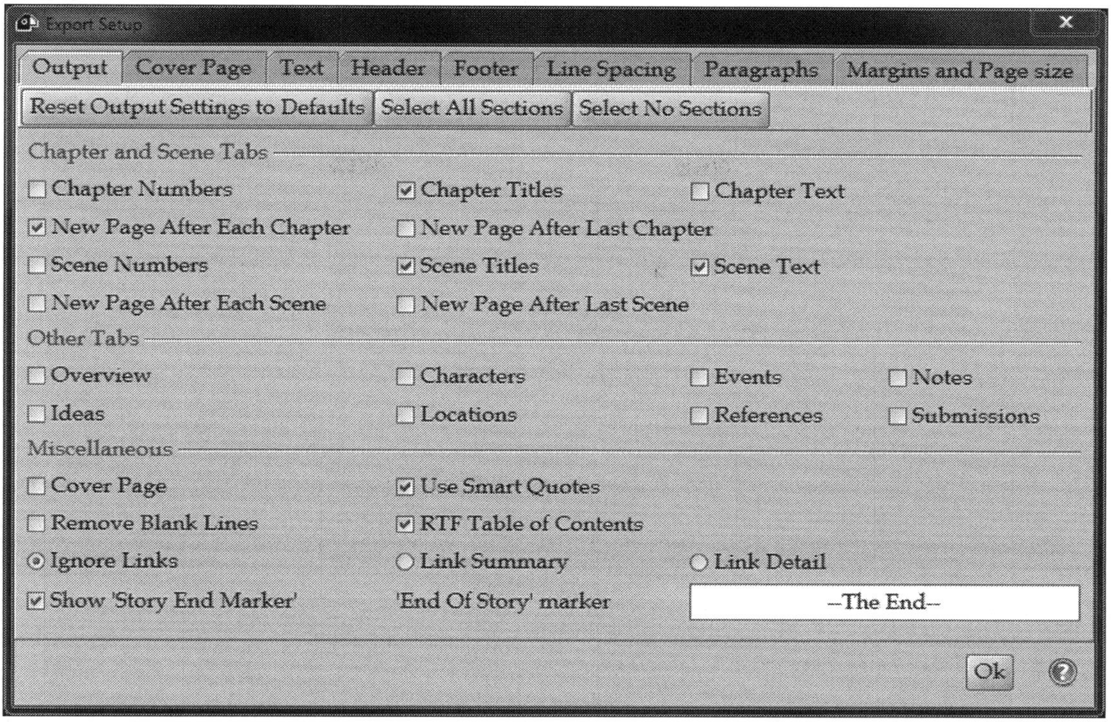

Figure 7.2 Export output options.

Export Output

In the export output, make sure you've checked some type of text. We didn't select chapter text (in Figure 7.2) because that prints chapter details text (where we recorded notes not intended for direct use in our story). Typically, you will want to export scene (and/or chapter) text only. However, if you are exporting in order to print and review everything you've written, then you can include text from other tabs. For example, you may want to review your character information.

If you used line breaks for new paragraphs (instead of indenting), then don't check Remove Blank Lines, or your story will run together with no breaks within scenes.

> *There is no one way to write.*
>
> —William S. Burroughs

Export Cover Page

You'll probably need to export a cover page only if you're sending your manuscript to someone. If you choose to export a cover page, it will automatically format as in Figure 7.3.

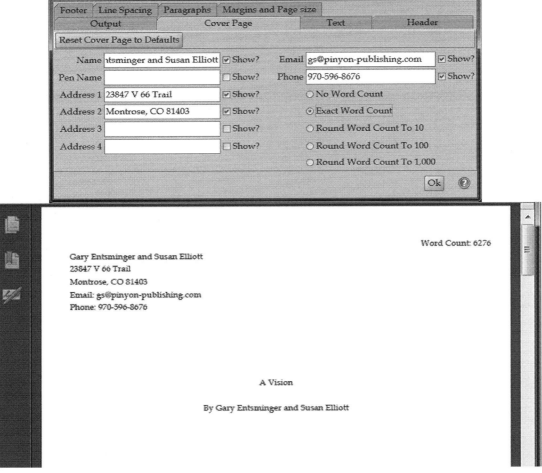

Figure 7.3 Export cover page options (*Top*) and output (*Bottom*).

Export Text

Choose a font style and size that you prefer for your export (Figure 7.4). The Main heading text applies to the chapter title. The Sub-heading text applies to the scene title. Normal text applies to the story text.

> *Let me inspect then the book itself. It must be nearly 500 pages by now. It started by saying, 'I'm going to tell you how things were then.' Now, has it done that? I don't know. I just don't know.*
>
> **—John Steinbeck**

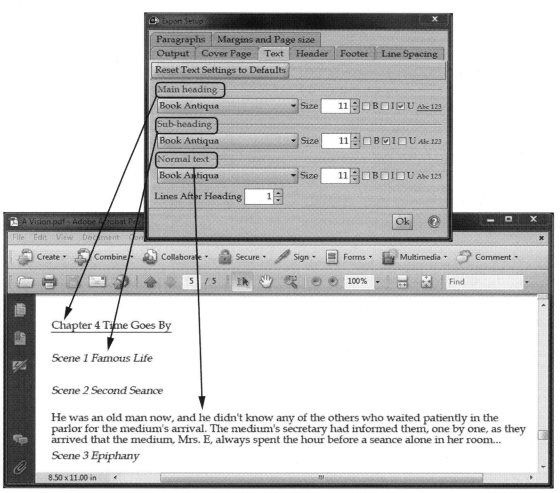

Figure 7.4 Export text options (*Above*) and output (*Below*).

Export Headers & Footers

Use headers and footers to label page numbers, chapter titles, story title, and/or author name (Figure 7.5). Options for what can appear in headers and footers are similar. Section Title refers to the Chapter Title. If you want scene titles in headers or footers, you can add them after the export.

The first page of a book is always a right-hand page. If you're exporting this book to self-publish, you will want to add other frontal matter, such as title pages, copyright page, and acknowledgements. It's best to add these pages after you export your main story from WriteItNow.

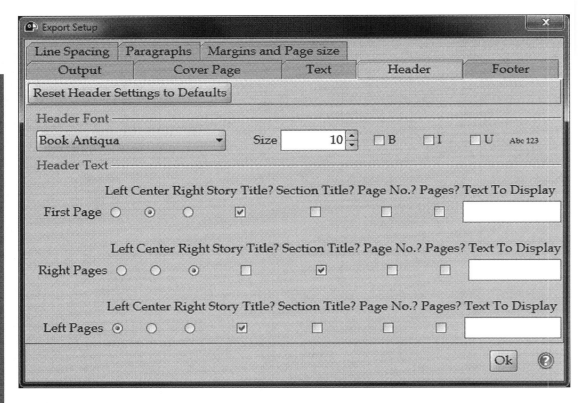

Figure 7.5 Export header options set to produce title on left pages (as well as very first right page) and scene (section) titles on right pages.

Export Line Spacing

The line spacing you choose will depend on where your export is headed. If you're going to self-publish your book, keep line spacing at 1x (Figure 7.6). If you're sending the manuscript to someone to read, give them more space (1.5x or 2x).

Export Paragraphs

Set the type of paragraphs you prefer. Justify the text if you want your text to look like a "book," where the text spreads all the way to the left and right margins (Figure 7.7). Don't have WriteItNow indent paragraphs if you've already added indents manually. If you manually indented a paragraph, WriteItNow will export it using your indents. If you haven't indented, WriteItNow will prefix the line with the number of spaces you specify in the Spaces To Indent Paragraphs box.

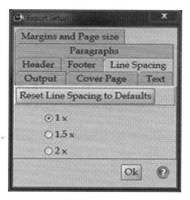

Figure 7.6 Export line spacing options.

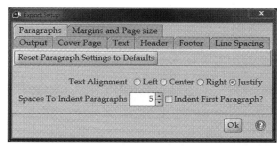

Figure 7.7 Export paragraph options.

> *Clutter is the disease of American writing. We are a society strangling in unnecessary words, circular constructions, pompous frills, and meaningless jargon.*
>
> —William Zinsser

EXPORT PARAGRAPHS

Export Margins & Page Size

Specify margins and page size. If you're exporting to submit to a publisher, you will probably want a classic page size, such as 8 1/2" x 11". If you're exporting to create an E-Book or to self-publish a book, you will want a standard book size, such as 6" x 9" (Figure 7.8). If you're planning to print and bind your book (*e.g.,* for self-publishing), then after you export, adjust the page layout for inside/outside margins instead of left/right margins. Make your inside margin larger to account for the space lost in a bound spine.

> If your purpose is to make a lot of money on a book or a film, there are certain rules to observe. You're aiming for the general public, and there are all sorts of things the general public just doesn't want to see or hear. A good rule is never expect a general public to experience anything they don't want to experience. You don't want to scare them to death, knock them out of their seats, and above all you don't want to puzzle them.
>
> —William S. Burroughs

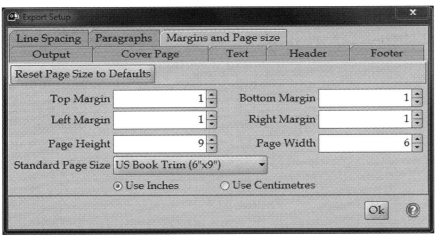

Figure 7.8 Export margins and page size options.

Export to Document

You can export your story to a completely new file that can be used by other programs. Your original .wnw file will still exist (and still be open) after you export to another file type.

You have the choice of exporting to four file types: .rtf, .pdf, .html, and .txt (Figure 7.9). For PC users, when you export to one of these file types, the default program (as set on your computer) for using these types of files will automatically open and load the exported file. Mac users should run their preferred program and load the exported file.

By default, WriteItNow will name the exported file for you. If your story title contains characters that are not valid in a file name, WriteItNow will convert them to spaces. For example, WriteItNow would save "Westward Ho!" as "Westward Ho .txt."

If you want control over naming exported files, from the Main menu, select Settings > Tool Settings > Set Export Filename. The next time you export, WriteItNow will ask you for a file name.

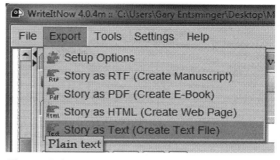

Figure 7.9 Export to navigation.

EXPORT FILE TYPES

.rtf   load your story in a word processor like Microsoft Word.

.pdf   create an E-Book

.html   create a file to use as a webpage

.txt   read and edit your file with a text editor (no links or formatting: bold, italic, underline)

Submissions

Now that you know how to export your WriteItNow story, you may want to submit it to an editor, reviewer, or publisher. Keep track of your submissions in the Submissions tab.

When you click the Submissions tab, first add an entry by clicking the ⊞ button (Figure 7.10A). The window will expand, providing places to add submissions details. Use the editor window to make notes to yourself or copy and paste a submission letter you sent out (Figure 7.10C).

Record when you sent in the submission (Figure 7.10D). When you get a reply, record the reply date and the general result using the drop down (Accepted, Rejected, Rewrite requested) (Figure 7.10D). When your story gets published, record when it was published and when you received advance payments or royalties and how much (Figure 7.10E).

You can export submissions details from the Options button (Figure 7.10B).

And while you're waiting for the money to roll in, start a new story. Happy writing.

SUBMISSIONS

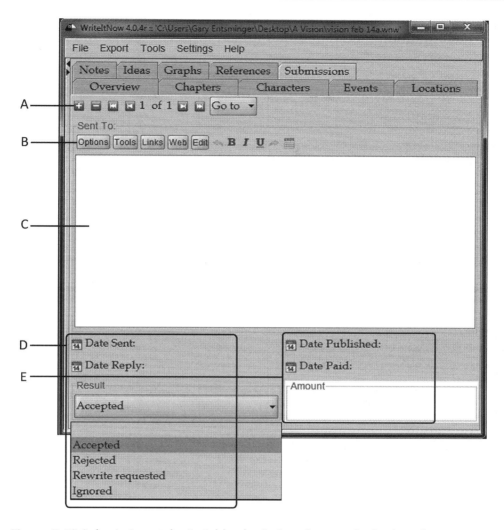

Figure 7.10 Submissions tab. **A.** Add submissions button, **B.** Options for export, **C.** Editor window for notes, **D.** Submission records, and **E.** Publication records.

Hot Key Shortcuts

Table 8.1 Hot key Shortcuts.

Ctrl+Z	Undo		Ctrl+W	Section Word Count
Ctrl+Y	Redo		Ctrl+L	Spelling Checker
Ctrl+A	Select All		Ctrl+T	Thesaurus for Selected Text
Ctrl+C	Copy		Ctrl+Q	Readability of Section
Ctrl+V	Paste		Alt+L	File Load
Ctrl+X	Cut Selected Text		Ctrl+S	File Save
Ctrl+F	Find Text		Alt+A	File Save As
Ctrl+R	Replace Text		Alt+N	Create New Story
Ctrl+M	Import Plain Text		Alt+W	Web Link
Ctrl+B	Bold		Alt+F	File Link
Ctrl+I	Italic		Ctrl+1	Add Chapter Link
Ctrl+U	Underline		Ctrl+2	Add Scene Link
Ctrl+Home	Goto Text Start		Ctrl+3	Add Character Link
Ctrl+End	Goto Text End		Ctrl+4	Add Event Link
Ctrl+P	Go Up One Line		Ctrl+5	Add Location Link
Ctrl+N	Go Down One Line		Ctrl+6	Add Idea Link
Ctrl+K	Show Accent Dialog		Ctrl+7	Add Note Link
Ctrl+F1	Story Word Count		Ctrl+8	Add Reference Link
Ctrl+F2	Story Readability		Alt+Shift+S	Web Search for Text
Ctrl+F4	Thesaurus		Alt+Shift+I	Web Search for Images
Ctrl+F5	Story Board		Alt+Shift+D	Web Search for Dictionary
Ctrl+F6	Writing Targets		Alt+Shift+T	Web Search for Thesaurus
Ctrl+F7	Create Random Character		Alt+Shift+E	Web Search for Encyclopedia
Ctrl+F8	Create Character from Add-On		Alt+Shift+Q	Web Search for Quote
Ctrl+F9	Use Prompt Set		Alt+Shift+R	Web Search for Rhyme
Ctrl+Shft+F9	Edit Prompt Set		Alt+F4	Exit Program
Ctrl+F10	Global Find			
Ctrl+F11	Global Replace			
Ctrl+F12	Update Relationships			

Recommended Reading

Bradbury, Ray. Zen in the Art of Writing. Joshua Odell Editions. 1994.

Brande, Dorethea. Becoming a Writer. Harcourt, Brace and Company. 1934.

Burroughs, William S. The Adding Machine. Arcade Publishing. 1985.

Dillard, Annie. The Writing Life. HarperPerennial. 1990.

Fickett, Harold. "Gushers and Bleeders," *in* Syllable of Water. Paraclete Press. 2008.

Gardner, John. The Art of Fiction. Vintage Books. 1984.

Goldberg, Natalie. Writing Down the Bones. Shambhala. 1986.

Handke, Peter. The Afternoon of a Writer. Translated by Ralph Manheim. Minerva. 1991.

Hobson, Archie, Ed. The Oxford Dictionary of Difficult Words. Oxford U. 2001.

King, Stephen. On Writing. Pocket. 2002.

Lamott, Anne. Bird by Bird: Some Instructions on Writing and Life. Anchor. 1995.

Magee, Rosemary M. Conversations with Flannery O'Connor. University Press of Mississippi. 1987.

Mathieu, W.A. The Listening Book. Shambhala. 1991.

Powys, John Cowper. A Philosophy of Solitude. Simon and Schuster. 1933.

Shaw, Luci. Breath for the Bones: Art, Imagination, and Spirit. Thomas Nelson. 2007.

Steinbeck, John. Journal of a Novel. The Viking Press. 1969.

The Chicago Manual of Style. 15th Edition. U. of Chicago Press. 2003.

Welty, Eudora. On Writing. Modern Library. 2002.

William Strunk Jr. and E.B. White. The Elements of Style, Third Edition. MacMillan Publishing Co. 1979.

Woolf, Virginia. The Common Reader. Harcourt, Brace. 1925.

Zinsser, William. On Writing Well. Harper and Row. 1980.

Index

7298715R0

Made in the USA
Lexington, KY
08 November 2010